Christian Jr./Sr High School
2100 Greenfield Dr.
El Cajon, CA 92019

1st EDITION

Perspectives on Modern World History

The Bosnian Conflict

1st EDITION

Perspectives on Modern World History

The Bosnian Conflict

Alexander Cruden

Editor

GREENHAVEN PRESS
A part of Gale, Cengage Learning

GALE
CENGAGE Learning

Detroit • New York • San Francisco • New Haven, Conn • Waterville, Maine • London

Elizabeth Des Chenes, *Managing Editor*

© 2012 Greenhaven Press, a part of Gale, Cengage Learning.

Gale and Greenhaven Press are registered trademarks used herein under license.

For more information, contact:
Greenhaven Press
27500 Drake Rd.
Farmington Hills, MI 48331-3535
Or you can visit our Internet site at gale.cengage.com.

For product information and technology assistance, contact us at
Gale Customer Support, 1-800-877-4253.

For permission to use material from this text or product, submit all requests online at
www.cengage.com/permissions.

Further permissions questions can be e-mailed to permissionrequest@cengage.com.

Articles in Greenhaven Press anthologies are often edited for length to meet page requirements. In addition, original titles of these works are changed to clearly present the main thesis and to explicitly indicate the author's opinion. Every effort is made to ensure that Greenhaven Press accurately reflects the original intent of the authors. Every effort has been made to trace the owners of copyrighted material.

Cover image © Roger Hutchings/In Pictures/Corbis.

LIBRARY OF CONGRESS CATALOGING-IN-PUBLICATION DATA

The Bosnian conflict / Alexander Cruden, book editor.
    p. cm. -- (Perspectives on modern world history)
    Includes bibliographical references and index.
ISBN 978-0-7377-5786-6 (hardcover)
1. Yugoslav War, 1991–1995--Bosnia and Hercegovina. 2. Yugoslav War, 1991–1995--Atrocities. 3. Bosnia and Hercegovina--History--1992– 4. Bosnia and Hercegovina--Ethnic relations. I. Cruden, Alex.
    DR1313.3.B6637 2011
    949.703--dc23   2011023877

Printed in the United States of America
1 2 3 4 5 6 7 15 14 13 12 11

CONTENTS

Foreword   1

Introduction   4

World Map   9

CHAPTER 1   **Historical Background on the Bosnian Conflict**

1. An Overview of the Conflict in
   the Balkans   13

   Worldmark Encyclopedia of the Nations

   Yugoslavia broke apart in the 1980s, forming
   five republics, including Bosnia. Ethnic, religious, and nationalistic tensions arose in the
   region. Forces backed by Serbia and Croatia
   launched attacks on Bosnia in the early 1990s.

2. Centuries of Strife Set the Stage for
   the Bosnian Conflict   21

   Michael Cusack

   The Balkans has a centuries-old history of
   ethnic and religious violence. Fighting among
   Muslims and Christians began when Muslim
   Turks conquered the area in 1453 and contin-
   ues in modern times.

3. Humanitarian Aid Is Not Enough in
   a Time of Mass Killings   27

   Margaret Thatcher et al.

   Western countries need to do more than send
   aid, writes a group of prominent people from

across the globe to US president Bill Clinton and other heads of state. They say that the West must act immediately to stop the massacre of Bosnians.

4. The United States Aims to Facilitate Peace in the Balkans   **34**

Bill Clinton

Saying that stability in central Europe is vital to US interests, President Bill Clinton declares that the American ideals of liberty, democracy, and peace can and should be applied in Bosnia. As a result, he says he has committed US troops to join others from NATO as peacekeepers in the Balkans.

5. A Leader of Violence in the Balkans Dies Before Being Convicted   **46**

Marcus Tanner

The career of Serbian leader Slobodan Milosevic tells much of the story of the conflict in and around Bosnia. Finally brought to trial before a UN war crimes tribunal, Milosevic died before the trial concluded, remaining unrepentant all the way to his grave.

6. Fifteen Years Later, Serbia Condemns a Mass Slaughter   **52**

Ron Synovitz

Fifteen years after Serbian forces killed about eight thousand Bosnian Muslims in the single worst loss of life in the war, the Serbian parliament condemns the killings, expresses sympathy for victims, and apologizes for not doing enough to prevent the massacre.

CHAPTER 2   Controversies Surrounding the
Bosnian Conflict

1. Ethnic Conflict Was Not the Central
   Cause of the Strife in Bosnia   **60**

   Susan L. Woodward

   The belief that the conflict was rooted in ethnic hatred allowed it to last longer. The war's
   real origin was the erosion of government
   authority and economic pressures.

2. Religion Was the Main Issue Behind
   the Attacks in Bosnia   **71**

   Michael A. Sells

   The central goal of the Serbian attacks was
   to wipe out five hundred years of peaceful
   Christian and Muslim coexistence. "Ethnic
   cleansing" was, in fact, religious-based genocide carried out by Serbs and their Croatian
   allies.

3. The United States and Western Europe
   Mishandled the Outbreaks of Violence
   in Bosnia   **79**

   Lester H. Brune

   The seeds of war were sown during the
   administration of US president Ronald
   Reagan and grew as the administration of
   George H.W. Bush continued to maintain
   that problems in Yugoslavia should be
   addressed solely by Europeans.

4. Different US Strategies Could Have
   Limited the Damage   **93**

   Wayne Bert

   The United States could have committed
   troops earlier and prevented years of conflict

or could have given Bosnians resources to defend themselves. Instead, the West chose a middle course, with devastating results.

5. Systematic Rape Was a Serbian
   War Tactic   103

   M. Cherif Bassiouni and Marcia McCormick

   Rape and sexual violence were used to some degree as a war tactic by all sides in the conflict. But most of the victims were Bosnian Muslims and most of the perpetrators were Bosnian Christian Serbs.

6. A UN Declaration Failed to Save
   Thousands of Lives in Srebrenica   115

   Ivan Lupis

   A town in Bosnia that had been designated by the United Nations as a safe haven for Bosnian muslims instead became the site of the largest massacre in Europe since World War II.

7. The NATO Bombing Campaign Helped
   Bring Peace to the Balkans   126

   Ryan C. Hendrickson

   The NATO bombing campaign in Bosnia, though extremely controversial at the time, was a crucial step toward ending the war. It also began a wider role for the Western military alliance in European peacekeeping.

8. The NATO Bombing Hurt the Cause
   of the Bosnian People   136

   The Militant

   While claiming their aims were humanitarian, the United States and its allies were vying for imperialistic influence in the former

Yugoslavia. The bombing complicates matters for the working people of Bosnia in their struggle against the Serbian regime.

9. International Criminal Tribunals Are
Tools for Peace   **141**

Richard J. Goldstone

There would be much more violence in the world, including in the former Yugoslavia, without international criminal tribunals. They bring truth to light and protect innocent people from powerfully destructive forces.

10. The United States' Strategy Was
Correct for Bosnia, and for the Future   **151**

Richard Holbrooke

Bringing an end to the Bosnian war was an essential act for the interests of the United States. Peace was accomplished using both realism and idealism—a combination necessary for lasting success.

CHAPTER 3   Personal Narratives

1. Each Day Became Worse for a Girl
in Sarajevo   **161**

Zlata Filipović

In the spring of 1992, in Sarajevo, Bosnia, war shatters the life of a local thirteen-year-old girl from a middle-class family. The war rages through her street, her family, and her future. Each terrifying day she writes down the details of her hopes and fears.

2. Moral Bravery Persists Amid the
Desperation for Survival   **169**

Zlatko Dizdarevic

In Sarajevo, a city that not long before had hosted the Winter Olympics but was then torn by the horrors of open war, many people still strive to live with honor. And they do so in the face of abandonment by the international community.

3. The Contradictions of Bosnia Lead
   Toward Fear and Insanity   **182**

David Rieff

An American writer finds himself drawn deeply into the Bosnia war while the rest of the Western world distances itself from it. He sees—and is haunted by—the brutally fatal consequences of global hypocrisy.

4. A War Reporter Struggles to Remember
   and to Forget the Siege of Sarajevo   **194**

Janine di Giovanni

A war reporter finds Bosnia unlike any conflict about which she has reported before and a city where madness is the norm. She returns to Sarajevo years later and is struck by what has changed and what has not.

Chronology   **201**

For Further Reading   **206**

Index   **209**

FOREWORD

"History cannot give us a program for the future, but it can give us a fuller understanding of ourselves, and of our common humanity, so that we can better face the future."

—Robert Penn Warren,
American poet and novelist

The history of each nation is punctuated by momentous events that represent turning points for that nation, with an impact felt far beyond its borders. These events—displaying the full range of human capabilities, from violence, greed, and ignorance to heroism, courage, and strength—are nearly always complicated and multifaceted. Any student of history faces the challenge of grasping the many strands that constitute such world-changing events as wars, social movements, and environmental disasters. But understanding these significant historic events can be enhanced by exposure to a variety of perspectives, whether of people involved intimately or of ones observing from a distance of miles or years. Understanding can also be increased by learning about the controversies surrounding such events and exploring hot-button issues from multiple angles. Finally, true understanding of important historic events involves knowledge of the events' human impact—of the ways such events affected people in their everyday lives—all over the world.

Perspectives on Modern World History examines global historic events from the twentieth-century onward by presenting analysis and observation from numerous vantage points. Each volume offers high school, early college level, and general interest readers a thematically arranged anthology of previously published materials that address a major historical event, with an emphasis on international coverage. Each volume opens with background information on the event, then presents the controversies surrounding that event, and concludes with first-person narratives from people who lived through the event or were affected by it. By providing primary sources from the time of the event, as well as relevant commentary surrounding the event, this series can be used to inform debate, help develop critical thinking skills, increase global awareness, and enhance an understanding of international perspectives on history.

Material in each volume is selected from a diverse range of sources, including journals, magazines, newspapers, nonfiction books, personal narratives, speeches, congressional testimony, government documents, pamphlets, organization newsletters, and position papers. Articles taken from these sources are carefully edited and introduced to provide context and background. Each volume of Perspectives on Modern World History includes an array of views on events of global significance. Much of the material comes from international sources and from US sources that provide extensive international coverage.

Each volume in the Perspectives on Modern World History series also includes:

- A full-color **world map**, offering context and geographic perspective.
- An annotated **table of contents** that provides a brief summary of each essay in the volume.
- An **introduction** specific to the volume topic.
- For each viewpoint, a brief **introduction** that has notes about the author and source of the viewpoint, and that provides a summary of its main points.
- Full-color **charts**, **graphs**, **maps**, and other visual representations.

- Informational **sidebars** that explore the lives of key individuals, give background on historical events, or explain scientific or technical concepts.
- A **glossary** that defines key terms, as needed.
- A **chronology** of important dates preceding, during, and immediately following the event.
- A **bibliography** of additional books, periodicals, and websites for further research.
- A comprehensive **subject index** that offers access to people, places, and events cited in the text.

Perspectives on Modern World History is designed for a broad spectrum of readers who want to learn more about not only history but also current events, political science, government, international relations, and sociology—students doing research for class assignments or debates, teachers and faculty seeking to supplement course materials, and others wanting to improve their understanding of history. Each volume of Perspectives on Modern World History is designed to illuminate a complicated event, to spark debate, and to show the human perspective behind the world's most significant happenings of recent decades.

INTRODUCTION

One horrifying aspect of the conflict in Bosnia that raged from 1991 to 1995 was its ferociously personal nature. Longtime neighbors, acquaintances who had been in the same towns for decades, ethnic groups that had coexisted for centuries, suddenly were at each other's throats. People who had been citizens of the same nation savaged each other with massacres and mass rape of civilians as a war tactic.

After the years of fighting in this southeastern Europe region, no side was victorious. The conflict ended only because the United States and other major powers forced it to stop and then enforced peace for years. Even so, Bosnia, the nation in the center of the turmoil, remained territorially and governmentally divided among the combatant groups.

The Bosnian conflict might seem complex, yet its basics are clear. Before the fighting began, the area was governed by an adroit dictator familiarly known by a single name, Tito. A Communist, Tito came to power at the end of World War II. His country, Yugoslavia, was made up of Bosnia and five other territories: Serbia, Croatia, Slovenia, Macedonia, and Montenegro. Through the years, Tito was able to balance competing internal factions while also managing the rival influences of the world's superpowers.

After Tito's death in 1980, no one held Yugoslavia together. As its component territories moved toward becoming independent nations, ethnic, religious, nationalistic, and separatist interests undermined stability, as did power grabs by various individuals. Animosities with ancient roots burst forth. Fear and retaliation shattered tolerance and moderation. The tensions snapped into outright warfare in 1991, resulting in the killings of about one hundred thousand people and the displacement of an estimated 2 million.

Bosnia was in the middle of all of this. With a population mix that included, most prominently, Serbs and Muslims, Bosnia became the central battleground and a place of sieges, torture, defiance, and oppression.

The eventual peace settlement talks took place in Dayton, Ohio, shepherded by US officials. The negotiations were difficult and ultimately unsatisfactory to all parties, though they did end the armed conflict. The accord reached in 1995 set up two elected governments within Bosnia. One was a Bosnian-Croat federation, based in Bosnia's previous capital, Sarajevo. The other, slightly smaller in area, was Serb-dominated and known as Republika Srpska, based in the city of Banja Luka. Each had its own territory, president, legislature, police, and so on. In addition, the smaller separate district of Brčko was set up as a neutral area with authority shared by Bosnians, Serbs, and Croats. Placed over all of these entities was a nationwide Bosnian government with a presidency that rotated among members of each of the three main ethnic groups.

The chief result of this governmental structure has not been unity. Bosnian federation officials have continued their efforts to attain more authority for their side, while Serb officials sought to strengthen connections with neighboring Serbia. Some Croats within Bosnia actively favored creating a third entity. In 2007, the International Crisis Group, an independent organization drawn from almost fifty nationalities, said after a study that "Bosnia remains unready for unguided ownership of its own future—ethnic nationalism remains too strong."

This observation was reinforced by the 2008 election results, which divided sharply along ethnic lines. So did the elections of 2010, despite the efforts of some leaders to break the deadlock. For example, the mayor of Foca, a Serb-dominated city where large numbers of Bosnian Muslims had been raped and killed in the 1990s, campaigned on a platform of reconciliation. The mayor, Zdravko Krsmanovic, declared, "my mission is to promote peace, dialogue, compromise, and tolerance," reported Mark Lowen of BBC News on October 1, 2010. Krsmanovic encouraged mosques to be rebuilt and Bosnian Muslims to return. But a higher authority, Republika Srpska prime minister Milorad Dodok, devalued such efforts, telling Lowen that Bosnia was a "virtual, pointless country."

An October 3, 2010, a *New York Times* report on that year's elections quoted Anita Kapo, a twenty-two-year-old design student, as saying Bosnia was so paralyzed by nationalism that voting seemed futile. "I keep trying and trying and trying to be positive about Bosnia," she said. "But nothing ever changes."

The persistence of divisiveness in the country extended its negative effects even into the realm of the country's most popular sport. In the spring of 2011, Bosnia was suspended from world football (soccer) competition because its supervising body refused to consolidate its three-person presidency into a single position. The sports leadership mirrored the rotating presidency of the country, and that was unacceptable to the game's worldwide and European governing bodies.

More than fifteen years after the peace agreement was signed, two thousand European Union peacekeepers were still in Bosnia—evidence of the cease-fire's fragility. Little progress had been made, according to Martin Sletzinger, former director of the Woodrow Wilson Center's East European Studies program. In a 2011 *Wilson Quarterly* article, Sletzinger wrote: "The schisms that shattered Yugoslavia and unleashed civil war have been papered over but not resolved. . . . The nation-building efforts that resulted [from the 1995 peace agreement] are faltering, especially in Bosnia, where the United States has spent more than $2 billion on various aid, institution-building, and reconciliation efforts since 1993."

A major factor in the discord is Serbian resentment. For centuries, Serbs had fairly regarded themselves as the most substantial defenders of the region, the ones most effective against invaders. After Yugoslavia came apart, when Serb homelands and shrines were attacked, and in particular when Serbia's capital, Belgrade, was bombed by NATO in 1999, Serbs felt themselves unfairly cast by Western countries as villains. They also strongly resented the West's eagerness to recognize the region of Kosovo as a separate nation because Kosovo, long a part of Serbia, had great historic and religious significance for Serbs. As Sletzinger wrote: "Serbia remains the single largest nation in the Balkans, even without the 1.8 million people of Kosovo, and most knowledgeable observers agree there will be no stability or security in the region until the Serbs' legitimate concerns are addressed."

The difficulties of addressing these concerns are immense, particularly because the Serbs did far more of the killing than any other group. Each side has justifiable demands regarding land and other rights that overlap and thus appear irreconcilable. Worse, the memories of neighbor-against-neighbor atrocities—and particularly of the bloodbaths euphemistically labeled "ethnic cleansing"—remain raw. In such a context, moderate leadership is easily cut down as naive and weak, and efforts to reach out to the other side can be seen as betrayal.

Some of the core issues that set off the armed conflict in 1991 remain unresolved and were actually worsened by the fighting. Ominously, the same ethnic and religious divisions remain to this day. Cate Malek wrote in www .BeyondIntractability.org in July 2005: "Muslim, Serbian and Croatian [communities] are teaching their children three different folk histories of the war. As the children age, these different stories could easily spark new violence."

The selections included in this volume illuminate not only what happened in the Bosnian conflict and why, but how a widespread and terrifyingly personal violence could erupt there once more.

World Map

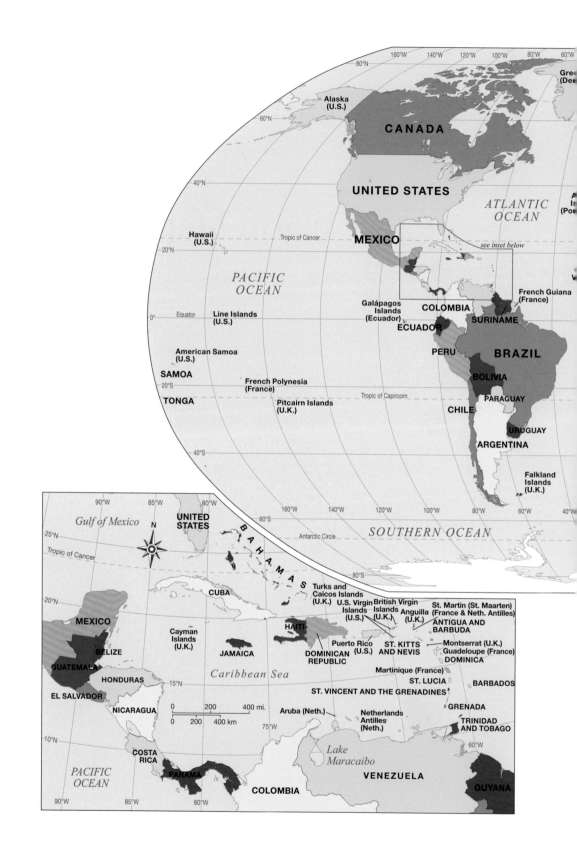

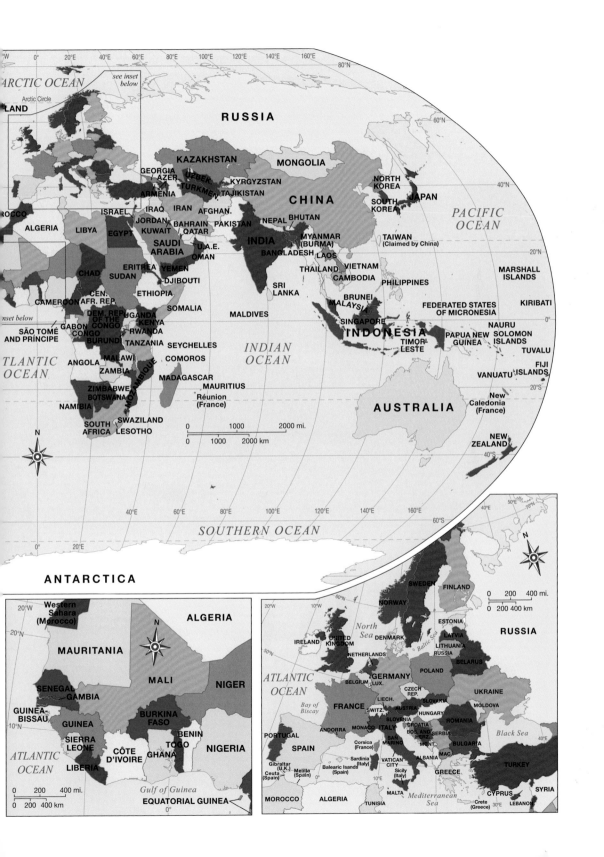

CHAPTER 1

Historical Background on the Bosnian Conflict

An Overview of the Conflict in the Balkans

Worldmark Encyclopedia of the Nations

As the following viewpoint notes, tensions spiked in and around Bosnia throughout the twentieth century, particularly among three groups: Serbs, Croatians, and Bosnian Muslims. From 1945 through the 1980s, the conflicting groups were all in one country, Yugoslavia. Beginning in 1991, different regions of the country declared independence, and fighting erupted within them. By far the worst violence took place in Bosnia (also known as Bosnia-Herzegovina), where Serbs attacked non-Serbs from 1992 to 1995. In addition, there was significant violence between Croats and Muslims. At the end of 1995, a US-negotiated truce led to an uneasy peace.

Photo on previous page: German soldiers serving in the NATO-led Stabilization Force in Bosnia walk in a devastated suburb of Sarajevo in 1998. (**AP Photo/Hidajet Delic.**)

SOURCE. *Worldmark Encyclopedia of the Nations*, "Bosnia-Herzegovina," v. 6: World Leaders 2003, 11th ed., pp. 77–81. Detroit: Gale, 2004. Copyright © Gale, a part of Cengage Learning, Inc. Reproduced by permission. www.cengage.com/permissions.

In 1908, the Austro-Hungarian empire formally annexed Bosnia. The move provoked neighboring Serbia, which coveted Bosnia because of its large Serbian population. When a young Bosnian Serb assassinated Austrian Crown Prince Ferdinand in Sarajevo in the name of Serbian national unity, World War I began. In 1918, Bosnia was incorporated into the newly formed Kingdom of Serbs, Croats, and Slovenes (later renamed Yugoslavia). During World War II, the Nazi puppet state in Croatia annexed all of Bosnia. This period saw mass murder of Serbs by the ruling Croatian fascists, as well as massacres of Muslims and Croats by Serb nationalists. The communist Partisans, led by Josip Broz, popularly known as "Tito," led the resistance. After the war, Bosnia-Herzegovina became one of six republics in the reconstituted Yugoslavia. Tito ruled from 1945 until his death in 1980.

In the 1980s, Bosnia, like the other republics, experienced rising anticommunist and nationalist sentiment. In 1990, a number of independent political parties were formed, including nationalist Muslim, Serb, and Croat parties. Multiparty elections were held in November 1990, based on a system of proportional representation by nationality. The nationalist parties ran on a platform of defense of their cultures, but none of them called for dismembering Bosnia. The election resulted in a Parliament divided along ethnic lines. The presidency of the republic included two members from each of the three ethnic groups, plus one ethnically mixed member. Alija Izetbegovic, head of the Democratic Action Party (SDA), was chosen to lead the presidency.

The three nationalist parties formed a coalition government. The Bosnian government at first did not seek independence but rather promoted remaining in a new Yugoslav federation. In March 1991, however, the presidents of Serbia and Croatia secretly agreed to partition Bosnia between them. By fall 1991, working closely with

MAP OF BOSNIA-HERZEGOVINA AND NEIGHBORING COUNTRIES

This map shows areas of the former Yugoslavia and surrounding countries. The different shading within Bosnia-Herzegovina shows the administrative divisions created by the Dayton Agreement of 1995.

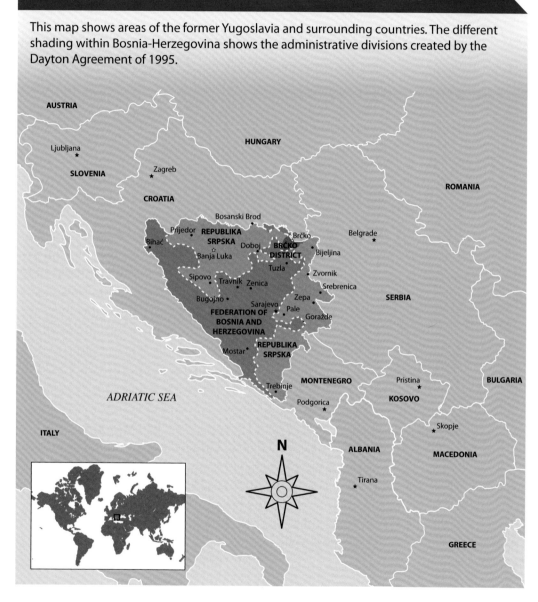

Belgrade, the Bosnian Serb Democratic Party (SDS) had established numerous "Serbian autonomous regions" throughout Bosnia and began forming its own militias. The SDS declared a "Serbian Republic of Bosnia and

> More than two million people were driven from their homes. . . . An estimated 200,000 persons were killed.

Herzegovina," uniting these regions. In January 1992, an independent Serb republic in Bosnia was created, claiming over 60% of the Republic's territory. Meanwhile, the European Union (EU) backed the idea of holding a referendum on independence as a preliminary move to international recognition. The Bosnian Muslim and Croat communities voted overwhelmingly in favor of independence, but the Bosnian Serb leadership called for a boycott of the vote.

Independence and Fighting Begin

In April 1992, Bosnia-Herzegovina gained recognition from the EU and the United States as an independent state. About the same time, Serbian irregular forces, backed by the Yugoslav Army, launched attacks throughout the republic. They quickly seized more than two-thirds of the Bosnian territory, carrying out policies of "ethnic cleansing" to drive non-Serb populations out of their territory. More than two million people were driven from their homes, creating the greatest flow of refugees in Europe since World War II (1939–45). An estimated 200,000 persons were killed. Fighting between ethnic Croats and Muslims in 1993–94 also resulted in "ethnic cleansing" by both sides. In response to U.S. and European pressure, Bosnian Croat and Muslim leaders agreed to a ceasefire between their communities and to the formation of a Muslim-Croat federation in Bosnia-Herzegovina. In this way, the Croat and Muslim communities were officially allied against their common Serb enemy.

Numerous international attempts to negotiate a peace settlement failed. United Nations (UN) peacekeepers on the ground, with a mandate to provide humanitarian aid to the victims of the war, were unable to keep the peace. In August 1995, a North Atlantic Treaty Organization

Marshal Tito ruled the six republics of Yugoslavia from 1945 until his death in 1980. **(Hulton Archive/ Getty Images.)**

(NATO) bombing campaign, coupled with a series of successful Muslim-Croat counteroffensives against the Bosnian Serb forces, brought the parties to the negotiating table. Serbian president Slobodan Milosevic accepted responsibility for the Bosnian Serb leadership. After three weeks of negotiations at Wright-Patterson Air Force Base in Dayton, Ohio, the presidents of Bosnia, Croatia, and Serbia agreed to a wide-reaching peace accord (known as the "Dayton Accords") in November 1995.

"Ethnic Cleansing" Is Not Clean

"Ethnic cleansing" is a loaded term. It implies that the object—a particular ethnic group—is tainted, dirty, inferior. Furthermore, it implies the group carrying out the action is on a morally superior mission.

The term was used frequently regarding the conflict in and around Bosnia in the early 1990s. One group tried to "cleanse" a territory by removing other groups, killing them or driving them out by force and terror, and erasing traces of their culture. Armed Serbs wanted much of Bosnia to be only Serbian; some Croatians tried to eliminate Serbs from certain areas, and so on.

In fact, none of the warring groups was clean, and the result of their so-called cleansing was widespread human devastation.

Although attempts by one ethnic group to remove another from an area are found throughout history, the first use of the term "ethnic cleansing" appears to have been reported in August 1991. A *Washington Post* article said: "The Croatian political and military leadership issued a statement Wednesday declaring that Serbia's 'aim is obviously the ethnic cleansing of the critical areas that are to be annexed to Serbia.'"

Genocide and ethnic cleansing are not quite the same. The former aims to destroy an ethnic, religious, or racial group through mass murder. The latter aims to remove a group from an area by any of several means, including killing.

Attempting to Impose a Postwar Structure

Under the terms of the Dayton peace agreement, Bosnia-Herzegovina maintains its current external borders. Internally, it comprises two equal entities, the Muslim-

Croat Federation and the Republika Srpska. Each entity has its own Parliament and government with wide-ranging powers, as well as its own armed forces. Each entity may establish "special parallel relationships with neighboring states," meaning Croatia and Serbia. At the all-republic level, there is a joint presidency, council of ministers, and a bicameral legislature.

Under the accords, the Muslim-Croat Federation received roughly 51% of the territory of Bosnia-Herzegovina while the Republika Srpska received 49%. The parties to the accords could not agree on who would control the Brcko region, a strategic northeastern corridor between the Serb-held regions. The status of Brcko was submitted to binding arbitration. In March 1999, a tribunal determined that Brcko would have its own multiethnic autonomous government. The military part of the Dayton accords committed the two sides to maintain the ceasefire and separate their forces. A NATO-led force was deployed to ensure implementation of the military section of the agreement. The accords required the parties to cooperate fully with the international war crimes tribunal for the former Yugoslavia. In 2001 and 2002, the tribunal began issuing indictments and arresting those charged with war crimes, including Slobodan Milosevic, Radovan Karadzic, and Ratko Mladic. The agreement included guarantees on the right of refugees to return to their homes and on the protection of human rights.

Implementation of the military aspects of the agreement proceeded smoothly, although NATO had to extend its initial one-year deployment numerous times. In June 1998, NATO pledged to keep its peacekeeping force in Bosnia until a self-sustaining peace is achieved. . . .

Joint Presidents Share Executive Duties

The joint presidency of Bosnia and Herzegovina consists of three members, one representing each of the country's three main ethnic constituencies (Bosniak, Serb, and Croat). Members are directly elected by voters in one of the country's two political entities (the Republika Srpska [RS] for the Serb member; the Bosnian Federation for the Muslim and Croat members). Chairmanship of the joint presidency rotates among the three members, with each occupying the post for eight months, during which time he is the country's official head of state.

The major presidential responsibilities are in the area of foreign policy and include relations with foreign countries and international organizations, appointment of ambassadors and other international representatives, negotiating treaties, and cooperation with nongovernmental organizations. The members of the presidency are also responsible for presenting an annual budget to Parliament and executing parliamentary decisions.

Centuries of Strife Set the Stage for the Bosnian Conflict

Michael Cusack

Ethnic and religious violence have been a part of Bosnian history since the Middle Ages, according to the following viewpoint. The Muslim presence in the region began in the middle of the 1400s, when the Ottoman Turks invaded. About four hundred years later, Russia began helping Serbian Christians take power. Over the centuries, the author explains, various acts of repression and violence primed the region for widespread conflict among its various ethnic groups. Michael Cusack writes about European history.

For more than 1,000 years, the Balkans were controlled by the Byzantine Empire, the eastern successor to the old Roman Empire and the cradle of the Christian Eastern Orthodox Church. It was during

SOURCE. Michael Cusak, "An Ancient Hatred," *Scholastic Update*, v. 126, no. 12, March 25, 1994, pp. 18–19. Used by permission of Scholastic, Inc.

these years that the Eastern Orthodox religion took firm root among the Serb population.

But Croatia and Slovenia were more influenced by the Italian city-state of Venice. Thus, Croats and Slovenes became Roman Catholics.

Adherents of the two opposing religions, living side by side, viewed each other as heretics—people who dissented from "true religion."

> The Ottomans slaughtered Serb nobles and gave their lands to Muslims, who treated the Christian peasants like slaves.

In 1453, the Byzantine empire fell to the Ottoman Turks. Catholics and Orthodox Christians joined together to resist the invading Muslims, but lost. As years went by, many Bosnians converted to the Islamic faith of their conquerors. Bosnians who remained loyal to the Eastern Orthodox faith despised those who converted to Islam. They called the Bosnian Muslims traitors, opportunists who had sided with the invaders.

In Serbia, hatred of Muslims was fierce. The Ottomans slaughtered Serb nobles and gave their lands to Muslims, who treated the Christian peasants like slaves. Numerous Serb revolts over the centuries were brutally put down.

Russia Backs Serbian Interests

In the early 19th century, Ottoman power began to decline and Russian influence began to rise. Like the Balkans, Russia consisted primarily of Slavs, or people whose language was rooted in the old Slavic tongue of Eastern Europe. Furthermore, Russia was dominated by the Eastern Orthodox Church. It saw itself as the champion of Christian Slavs suppressed by the Muslims.

A Russian victory against the Ottoman Empire in 1829 gained Serbia partial, then full, independence. Fearing that ethnic hatred in the Balkans could explode into a wider war, top European statesmen gathered in 1878 for a plan to bring peace. Out of the meeting, Bosnia and Herzegovina, with its substantial Serb population, became a semi-independent state under the protection of Austria-Hungary. But in 1908, Austria-Hungary put Bosnia under military rule. The move outraged Serbia.

On June 28, 1914, Archduke Franz Ferdinand, heir to the thrones of Austria and Hungary, was visiting the capital of Bosnia and Herzegovina. As he and his wife rode the streets of Sarajevo, a Serb nationalist assassinated them.

The killing was the spark that set Europe aflame. Blaming Serbia for the killings, Austria-Hungary declared war. Bound by treaty, the other nations of Europe jumped into the fray. World War I was under way.

In the early stages of the war, the army of Serbia was forced to retreat over the mountains into Greece. But the Serbs regrouped and went on to help the Allies—Britain, France, and the United States—defeat the German-led Central Powers and win World War I.

Serbs Become the Dominant Group

After World War I, the Allies united southern Slavs into one nation, forming the Kingdom of the Serbs, Croats, and Slovenes. As a reward for the help Serbia provided in helping to

ETHNIC BREAKDOWN IN YUGOSLAVIA AND BOSNIA

These charts reflect the way the residents of Yugoslavia as a whole and Bosnia in particular identified themselves in census documents. Some identified themselves as part of an ethnic or religious group; other simply described themselves as "Yugoslavs."

Yugoslavia in 1981

Others 8.1%
"Yugoslavs" 5.4%
Macedonians 6.0%
Albanians 7.7%
Slovenes 7.8%
Muslims 8.9%
Croats 19.8%
Serbs 36.3%

Bosnia in 1981

Others 8.4%
"Yugoslavs" 7.4%
Croats 17.2%
Muslims 37.0%
Serbs 30.0%

Taken from: Compiled by editor from national census studies.

> Alexander [king of Yugoslavia] scrapped the constitution in 1929 and made himself dictator. He . . . imprisoned political rivals without trial.

win the war, Peter I of Serbia was named king of the new nation.

Upon Peter's death in 1921, his son Alexander took the throne. Alexander placed Serbs in key positions throughout the kingdom, and favored the Eastern Orthodox religion over others. He also imposed one official language, Serbo-Croatian. Bosnians, Croats, and Slovenes strongly protested these moves, and began plotting to overthrow the monarchy.

In reaction, Alexander scrapped the constitution in 1929 and made himself dictator. He renamed the country Yugoslavia and imprisoned political rivals without trial, proving particularly brutal in suppressing Croat nationalism. Several leading Croats disappeared. Extremist Croats then formed a secret terrorist society, called the Ustache. In 1934, the Ustache assassinated Alexander. Alexander's son and heir, Peter II, was only 11 years old, so his cousin Prince Paul took power. Paul continued to enforce Alexander's unpopular policies.

At the outbreak of war [World War II], Yugoslavia was neutral, but Prince Paul favored Nazi Germany over the Allied nations of Britain and France. That angered Peter II, who fired Paul and took control.

In 1941, German troops invaded, forcing Peter II to flee. The Nazis gave rule of Croatia to the Ustache. The Ustache adopted a policy of genocide against Serbs, Jews, Gypsies, and other minorities living in Croatia and Bosnia. During this time, they killed hundreds of thousands of Serbs, fueling hatred between Croats and Serbs that continues to this day.

Two resistance armies developed in occupied Yugoslavia to fight back. One was loyal to Peter II; the other was headed by Josip Broz, a Croat and a Communist who called himself Tito. The two armies fought not only the

Germans, the Ustache, and other German collaborators, but each other as well.

Tito's army prevailed; by 1945, it controlled almost all of Yugoslavia.

Tito Held the Country Together

After the war, Tito formed the Federal Republic of Yugoslavia, in which six republics—Bosnia and Herzegovina, Croatia, Macedonia, Montenegro, Serbia, and Slovenia—had equal status. In reality, power was held by Tito, who suppressed any political opposition and ethnic hatreds.

Joseph Stalin, leader of the Soviet Union, sought to make Yugoslavia a puppet regime, as he did with other nations in Eastern Europe. But Tito successfully steered

Franz Ferdinand, the archduke of Austria, and his wife, Sophie, are seen in an open carriage shortly before their assassination, which sparked World War I. (Henry Guttmann/ Getty Images.)

Yugoslavia on an independent course, away from the Cold War between the U.S. and the U.S.S.R.

When Tito died in 1980, no one leader had the power to take his place. So a nine-member presidency was formed, in which each member served a rotating one-year term as president.

Under this clumsy arrangement, Communist power declined and regional and ethnic rivalries revived. In June 1991, Croatia and Slovenia declared their independence. Fighting broke out between the former republics of Croatia and Serbia. A few months later, Macedonia as well as Bosnia and Herzegovina declared their independence. In 1992, Serbia and Montenegro created a new Yugoslavia.

Humanitarian Aid Is Not Enough in a Time of Mass Killings

Margaret Thatcher et al.

The following selection is a letter sent by British prime minister Margaret Thatcher and more than a hundred other prominent people to US president Bill Clinton and other world leaders on September 1, 1993. The letter argues that Western countries must act militarily to prevent the further killing of Bosnians. Sending humanitarian aid and issuing empty threats to the Serb forces have not brought about peace, the authors assert. To ensure Bosnian human rights and survival, the United States should lead the West to employ the successful model of the 1991 Persian Gulf War, they state. Margaret Thatcher was prime minister of the United Kingdom from 1979 to 1990.

SOURCE. Margaret Thatcher, et al., "Bosnia and the Future of Ethnic Cleansing," *World Affairs*, v. 156, no. 2, Fall 1993, pp. 104–106. Used by permission.

British prime minister Margaret Thatcher and more than a hundred other prominent people sent a letter to US president Bill Clinton and others urging military intervention to stop the killings of Bosnians. **(Fairfax Media/Getty Images.)**

An Open Letter to President [Bill] Clinton and Other Western Heads of State:

In Bosnia, the situation goes from bad to worse. The people there are in despair about their future. They are victims of brutal aggression. But they are also the victims of the failure of the democracies to act.

Instead of opposing the acquisition of territory by force, the United Nations and the democracies have dispatched humanitarian assistance to Bosnia. But welcome as it is, this will not stop the massacres or halt the ethnic cleansing. Humanitarian aid will not protect the besieged children of Bosnia from being herded into Muslim ghettos or orphaned or maimed or slaughtered.

These could have been our children.

If we do not act, immediately and decisively, history will read that in the last decade of this century the democracies failed to heed its most unforgiving lesson: that unopposed aggression will be enlarged and repeated, that a failure of will by the democracies will strengthen and encourage those who gain territory and rule by force.

Dividing Bosnia Would Doom Muslims

In Bosnia the democracies have used the need to deliver humanitarian aid both to excuse their own inaction and to keep the recognized multiethnic state of Bosnia outgunned and therefore itself unable to protect its civilian centers from slaughter by a dictator bent on making a Greater Serbia. Western governments now vying publicly to save several hundred maimed Bosnian children will not escape the responsibility they assumed for the slaughter of hundreds of thousands of other children and their parents, when they refused to let an independent Bosnia defend itself.

Recently, the U.N. and EC [European Community] mediators, with U.S. support, threatened to withdraw humanitarian aid in order to coerce the Bosnian government into accepting violent changes in its borders and a partition into ethnically pure states, with Bosnia a set of widely dispersed, unarmed Muslim ghettos. But the U.N., the EC and the U.S. have continually condemned such changes and that partition as totally unacceptable. Such a partition, they've said, is unstable: It will mean still more killing, broken families, and the expulsion of millions at a time when Europe is closing its doors to refugees. If the fall of Sarajevo is a preface to a partition creating unarmed Muslim ghettos, it will be a preface also to further disasters, ethnic cleansing and instability—in Sarajevo itself and other Bosnian "safe havens" protected only by the U.N., in the rest of the Balkans, and beyond.

Bosnia, unlike Somalia, was no civil war. Like Kuwait, it was a case of clear-cut aggression against a member of the U.N.—a member whose independence the U.S., Europe and the international community have recognized for at least 16 months.

When the Baath dictatorship seized all of Kuwait in August 1990, it tried to erase Kuwaiti identity using rape, torture, the seizure of Kuwaiti passports and the forging of a new identity of Kuwait as a province of Iraq. A coalition of several NATO powers and some non-NATO countries joined the U.S. in demanding and then, in January 1991, compelling Iraq's withdrawal by using first airpower throughout Iraq and then ground forces in Kuwait and southern Iraq. The coalition was excercising the right of individual and collective self-defense of each of its members and of Kuwait. It aimed at more than mitigating Kuwait's suffering. The U.N. endorsed the coalition's aim to get Iraq out of Kuwait, and the aims beyond Kuwait to reduce Iraq's power to terrorize its neighbors. But the U.N. exercised no authority over the coalition.

In the same way, the U.S. should now lead a coalition of Western governments that exercises the right of each to individual and collective self-defense. The U.N. Charter does not confer that right; it acknowledges it to be "inherent." Nor is that right conditioned on the secretary-general's approval.

The West's air-to-air fighters overflying Bosnia needed no further preparations to shoot down the command helicopters and helicopter gunships the Serbs, in yet another blatant violation of their promises, used to drive the Bosnian army from their defenses of Sarajevo on Mounts Igman and Bjelasnica. The West could have done this without

> Western governments should act now substantially to reduce Serbia's immediate and future power of aggression.

elaborate plans to coordinate air strikes against ground targets, without endangering U.N. forces on the ground, and without the permission of the secretary-general, Europe's Council of Ministers, the 16 NATO ambassadors and a variety of U.N. commanders—procedures that appear designed to make the fall of Sarajevo a fait accompli. A disaster not only for the Bosnians, but for the relevance of the U.N., Europe, NATO—and the U.S.

Western governments should act now substantially to reduce Serbia's immediate and future power of aggression and ultimately to put the Bosnians in a position where they won't have to rely indefinitely on the protection of the international community.

With this limited political aim, Western air power would play a much larger role, and U.S. and other Western ground forces a much smaller and more transient role, than in U.N.-directed options that look toward an indefinite future of protecting on the ground helpless Muslim ghettos and besieged corridors of supply to them. The ghettos and corridors to them would be subject to continuing artillery, armor and sniper attacks so long as the source of these attacks in Serbia is left intact.

Air power directed against the present and future potential sources of such attack can be used selectively and discriminately. The no-fly zone could be enforced and defenses suppressed over Serbia as well as Bosnia. And a very high percentage of the military aircraft on the large airfields in Serbia could be destroyed, with minimal danger to Serbian civilians or to UNPROFOR [UN Protection Force] troops.

The U.N. alternatives mean a future of ethnic cleansing and endless military protection by the international community.

Late Action Is Better Than None

What the West says and does now in Bosnia will affect the future in Bosnia itself; in the rest of the Balkans; and in other newly independent countries that, having gained their freedom when a communist dictatorship fell apart, now find that freedom threatened by former rulers who would, like [Slobodan] Milosevic, use the pretext of protecting minorities to retake strategic facilities and territory their pan-national military have never been reconciled to giving up.

> The West can improve the odds for the survival of a free multiethnic Bosnia.

Even now, after 16 months of a perverse Western policy piously condemning the pan-Serbian aggressors while doing nothing to stop the massacres, the West can use military force substantially and discriminately to reduce the power of the poorly motivated and ill-disciplined Serbian Army in Bosnia and its source of support in Serbia itself. And the West can help arm the larger, highly motivated Bosnian Army that still maintains a precarious control of the towns containing most of Bosnia's industry, including its weapons industry. In this way the West can improve the odds for the survival of a free multiethnic Bosnia.

On the other hand, if Western mediators and UN-PROFOR confine unarmed Bosnian Muslims to small, purified remnants of Bosnia, the public will watch with horror as these ghettos disappear before its eyes on television while Serbs violate this ceasefire—as they have all the others for 23 months in Croatia and Bosnia. A spectacular display, at the same time, of the unshakably naive faith in Serbian promises that underlies Western cynicism. Realpolitik [practical politics] revealed as fantasy in real time.

Even if, like Kuwait in August 1990, all Bosnia (and not just Sarajevo) were seized, it would be essential for the democracies to make clear, as they did in the case of Kuwait, that violent border changes and ethnic cleansing will not stand, whether by Serbia in Croatia and Bosnia, or by Croatia in Bosnia.

If the West does not make that clear, it will have nothing persuasive to say to the Croats and the Serbs who have already renewed the conflict Serbia started two years ago when it used the Yugoslavian Army to seize territory in Croatia and then turned to invading Bosnia. Nor will the West be able to stop Serbian ethnic cleansing of Albanians in Kosovo and of Hungarians in Vojvodina. In Macedonia (unrecognized by either the U.S. or Europe because the Greeks object), where the U.S. and Sweden have deployed ground forces with no clear purpose, Western policy seems even murkier than for the other former Yugoslavian republics. There the West will have nothing coherent to say to resolve potential conflicts among Greeks, Serbs, Albanians, Bulgarians, Turks, and frustrated Macedonian nationalists who may topple the moderate [Kiro] Grigorov. Finally, the West will have nothing to say to discourage the now serious threat presented by pan-nationalists in the former Soviet Union and elsewhere.

Empty threats have a perverse effect.

Against a dictator who will yield only to superior force the West can threaten most ferociously in the hope that threats alone will be enough to stop aggression—that its threats and endless preparations will "send a message." But if the West doesn't use force at all or if it uses it symbolically rather than substantially to reduce Milosevic's power, or if it uses force to coerce Bosnian capitulation, "the message" received will only bring American and Western resolve into contempt.

The United States Aims to Facilitate Peace in the Balkans

Bill Clinton

Peace in Bosnia is crucial for US interests, President Bill Clinton says in the following viewpoint. In addition, it is possible and it is just for the United States to help Bosnians achieve the American ideals of liberty and democracy. After the cease-fire accord negotiated in Dayton, Ohio, Clinton announces on November 27, 1995, that the United States will send troops to Bosnia to join others from NATO as peacekeepers in the region. Bill Clinton was the forty-second president of the United States, serving from 1993 to 2001.

Photo on following page: US president Bill Clinton visits troops in Tuzla, Bosnia, on January 13, 1996. They had recently arrived to join the NATO peace-keepers. (Laurent Van Der Stockt/Gamma-Rapho via Getty Images.)

L ast week, the warring factions in Bosnia reached a peace agreement as a result of our efforts in Dayton, Ohio, and the support of our European and Russian partners. Tonight [November 27, 1995], I

SOURCE. Bill Clinton, "Why We're Sending Troops to Bosnia," address to the nation, November 27, 1995. www.dtic.mil/bosnia/army/pres_bos.html.

want to speak with you about implementing the Bosnian peace agreement and why our values and interests as Americans require that we participate.

Let me say at the outset: America's role will not be about fighting a war; it will be about helping the people of Bosnia to secure their own peace agreement. Our mission will be limited, focused, and under the command of an American general. In fulfilling this mission, we will have the chance to help stop the killing of innocent civilians . . . and at the same time to bring stability to central Europe—a region of the world that is vital to our national interests.

It is the right thing to do.

From our birth, America has always been more than just a place. America has embodied an idea that has become the ideal for billions of people throughout the world. Our founders said it best: America is about life, liberty and the pursuit of happiness. In this century especially, America has done more than simply stand for these ideas—we have acted on them and sacrificed for them. Our people fought two world wars so that freedom could triumph over tyranny.

After World War I, we pulled back from the world, leaving a vacuum that was filled by the forces of hatred. After World War II, we continued to lead the world. We made the commitments that kept the peace, that helped to spread democracy, that created unparalleled prosperity, and that brought victory in the Cold War.

The United States' Vital Interests Extend Beyond Its Borders

Today, because of our dedication, America's ideals— liberty, democracy and peace—are more and more the aspirations of people everywhere in the world. It is the power of our ideas—even more than our size, our wealth and our military might—that makes America a uniquely trusted nation.

With the Cold War over, some people now question the need for our continued active leadership in the world. They believe that, much like after World War I, America can now step back from the responsibilities of leadership. They argue that to be secure, we need only to keep our borders safe, and that the time has come now to leave to others the hard work of leadership beyond our borders.

> Problems that start beyond our borders can quickly become problems within them.

I strongly disagree.

As the Cold War gives way to the global village, our leadership is needed more than ever, because problems that start beyond our borders can quickly become problems within them.

We are all vulnerable to the organized forces of intolerance and destruction—terrorism, ethnic, religious and regional rivalries, the spread of organized crime and weapons of mass destruction, and drug trafficking.

Just as surely as fascism and communism, these forces also threaten freedom and democracy, peace and prosperity—and they too demand American leadership.

But nowhere has the argument for our leadership been more clearly justified than in the struggle to stop or prevent war and civil violence—from Iraq to Haiti, from South Africa to Korea, from the Middle East to Northern Ireland. We have stood up for peace and freedom because it is in our interest to do so and because it is the right thing to do.

The United States Must Take Action at Times

Now, that doesn't mean we can solve every problem. My duty as president is to match the demands for American leadership to our strategic interests and to our ability to make a difference. America cannot and must not be the world's policeman. We cannot stop war for all time, but we can stop some wars. We cannot save all women and all children, but we can save many of them. We can't do everything, but we must do what we can.

There are times and places where our leadership can mean the difference between peace and war, and where we can defend our fundamental values as a people and serve our most basic strategic interests. My fellow Americans, in this new era, there are still times when America—and America alone—can and should make the difference for peace.

> Nowhere today is the need for American leadership more stark or more immediate than in Bosnia.

The terrible war in Bosnia is such a case. Nowhere today is the need for American leadership more stark or more immediate than in Bosnia.

For nearly four years, a terrible war has torn Bosnia apart. Horrors that we prayed had been banished from Europe forever have been seared into our minds again. Skeletal prisoners caged behind barbed-wire fences, women and girls raped as a tool of war, defenseless men and boys shot down into mass graves, evoking visions of World War II concentration camps and endless lines of refugees marching into a future of despair.

When I took office, some were urging immediate intervention in the conflict. I decided that American ground troops should not fight a war in Bosnia, because the United States could not force peace on Bosnia's warring ethnic groups: the Serbs, Croats and Muslims.

Instead, America has worked with our European allies in searching for peace, stopping the war from spreading, and easing the suffering of the Bosnian people.

We imposed tough economic sanctions on Serbia. We used our air power to conduct the longest humanitarian air lift in history and to enforce a "no fly" zone that took the war out of the skies. We helped to make peace between two of the three warring parties: the Muslims and the Croats.

With Allies, Americans Turned the Tide

But as the months of war turned into years, it became clear that Europe alone could not end the conflict. This summer, Bosnian Serb shelling turned Bosnia's playgrounds and marketplaces into killing fields. In response, the United States led NATO's heavy and continuous air strikes—many of them flown by skilled and brave American pilots.

Those air strikes, together with the renewed determination of our European partners and the Bosnian Croat gains on the battlefield, convinced the Serbs, finally, to start thinking about making peace.

At the same time, the United States initiated an intensive diplomatic effort that forged a Bosnia-wide cease-fire and got the parties to agree to the basic principles of peace. Three dedicated American diplomats—Bob Frasure, Joe Kruzel, and Nelson Drew—lost their lives in that effort. Tonight we remember their sacrifice and that of their families. And we will never forget their exceptional service to the nation.

> America has a responsibility . . . to help turn this moment of hope into an enduring reality.

Finally, just three weeks ago, the Muslims, Croats and Serbs came to Dayton, Ohio—in America's heartland—to negotiate a settlement. There, exhausted by war, they made a commitment to peace. They agreed to put down their guns, to preserve Bosnia as a single state, to investigate and prosecute war criminals, to protect the human rights of all citizens, to try to build a peaceful, democratic future.

And they asked for America's help as they implement their agreement.

America has a responsibility to answer that request, to help turn this moment of hope into an enduring reality. To do that, troops from our country and around the world would go into Bosnia to give them the confidence they need to implement their peace plan. I refused to send American troops to fight a war in Bosnia, but I believe we must help to secure the Bosnian peace.

A Peaceful Bosnia Is a Crucial Need

I want you to know tonight what is at stake, exactly what our troops will be asked to accomplish, and why we must carry out our responsibility to implement the peace agreement.

Implementing the peace agreement in Bosnia can end the terrible suffering of the people—the warfare, the mass executions, the ethnic cleansing, the campaigns of rape and terror. Let us never forget a quarter of a million men, women and children have been shelled, shot and tortured to death. Two million people, half of the population, were forced from their homes and into a miserable life as refugees. These faceless millions hide millions of real personal tragedies.

For each of the war's victims was a mother or a daughter, a father or a son, a brother or a sister.

Now the war is over. American leadership created a chance to secure the peace and stop the suffering.

Securing the peace in Bosnia will also help build a free and stable Europe. Bosnia lies at the very heart of Europe, next door to many of its fragile new democracies and some of our closest allies.

Generations of Americans have understood that Europe's freedom and Europe's stability are vital to our own national security. That's why we fought two world wars in Europe. That's why we launched the Marshall Plan to restore Europe. That's why we created NATO and waged the Cold War. And that's why we must help the nations of Europe end their worst nightmare since World War II—now.

Without NATO Action, War Will Resume

The only force capable of getting this job done is NATO, the powerful military alliance of democracies that has guaranteed our security for half a century. Now as NATO's leader, and as the primary broker of the peace agreement, the United States must be an essential part of the mission.

If we're not there, NATO will not be there. The peace will collapse. The war will reignite. The slaughter of innocents will begin again. A conflict that already has claimed so many victims could spread like poison throughout the region, eat away at Europe's stability and erode our partnership with our European allies. And America's commitment to leadership will be questioned if we refuse to participate in implementing a peace agreement we brokered in the United States, especially since the presidents of Bosnia, Croatia and Serbia all asked us to participate and all pledged their best efforts to secure the security of our troops.

> Many other nations who share our goals will share our burdens.

When America's partnerships are weak and our leadership is in doubt, it undermines our ability to secure our interests and to convince others to work with us. If we do maintain our partnerships and our leadership, we need not act alone.

As we saw in the Gulf war and in Haiti, many other nations who share our goals will share our burdens. But when America does not lead, the consequences can be very grave—not only for others, but eventually for us as well.

As I speak to you, NATO is completing its planning for I-FOR, an international force for peace in Bosnia of about 60,000 troops. Already, more than 25 other nations, including our major NATO allies, have pledged to take part. They will contribute about two-thirds of the implementation force, some 40,000 troops. The United States would contribute the rest, about 20,000 soldiers.

A Precise Mission Will Minimize Risks

Later this week, the final NATO plan will be submitted to me for review and approval. Let me make clear what I expect it to include, and what it must include for me to give final approval to the participation of our armed forces.

First, the mission will be precisely defined, with clear, realistic goals that can be achieved in a definite period of time. Our troops will make sure each side withdraws its forces behind the front lines, and keeps them there. They will maintain the cease-fire to prevent the war from accidentally starting again. These effects, in turn, will help create a secure environment so that the people in Bosnia can return to their homes, vote in free elections and begin to rebuild their lives. Our Joint Chiefs of Staff have concluded that this mission should—and will—take about one year.

Second, the risks to our troops will be minimized. American troops will take their orders from the American general who commands NATO. They will be heavily armed and thoroughly trained. By making an overwhelming show of force, they will lessen the need to use force. But unlike the U.N. forces, they will have the authority to respond immediately—and the training and equipment to respond with overwhelming force—to any threat to their own safety or any violations of the military provisions of the peace agreement.

If the NATO plan meets with my approval, I will immediately send it to Congress and request its support. I will also authorize the participation of a small number of American troops in a NATO advance mission that will lay the groundwork for I-FOR—starting sometime next week. They will establish headquarters and set up the sophisticated communications systems that must be in place before NATO can send its troops, tanks and trucks to Bosnia. The implementation force itself would begin deploying in Bosnia in the days following the formal signature of the peace agreement in mid-December.

Other Nations and Agencies Will Join In

The international community will help to implement arms control provisions of the agreement so that future hostilities are less likely and armaments are limited, while the world community—the United States and others—makes sure the Bosnian Federation has the means to defend itself once I-FOR withdraws.

I-FOR will not be a part of this effort. Civilian agencies from around the world will begin a separate program of humanitarian relief and reconstruction, principally paid for by our European allies and other interested countries. This effort is absolutely essential to making peace endure. It will bring the people of Bosnia the food, shelter, clothing and medicine so many have been denied for so long. It will help them to rebuild—to rebuild their roads and their schools, their power plants and hospitals, their factories and shops.

It will reunite children with their parents, and families with their homes. It will allow the Bosnians freely to choose their own leaders. It will give all the people of Bosnia a much greater stake in peace than war, so that peace takes on a life and a logic of its own.

In Bosnia, we can and will succeed, because our mission is clear and limited. And our troops are strong and very well prepared. But my fellow Americans, no deployment of American troops is risk free, and this one may well involve casualties. There may be accidents in the field or incidents with people who have not given up their hatred. I will take every measure possible to

> Anyone—anyone—who takes on our troops will suffer the consequences. We will fight fire with fire—and then some.

minimize these risks, but we must be prepared for that possibility.

As president, my most difficult duty is to put the men and women who volunteer to serve our nation in harm's way when our interests and values demand it. I assume full responsibility for any harm that may come to them. But anyone contemplating any action that would endanger our troops should know this: America protects its own. Anyone—anyone—who takes on our troops will suffer the consequences. We will fight fire with fire—and then some.

After so much bloodshed and loss, after so many outrageous acts of inhuman brutality, it will take an extraordinary effort of will for the people of Bosnia to pull themselves from their past and start building the future of peace.

But with our leadership and the commitment of our allies, the people of Bosnia can have the chance to decide their future in peace. They have a chance to remind the world that, just a few short years ago, the mosques and churches of Sarajevo were a shining symbol of multiethnic tolerance—that Bosnia once found unity in its diversity.

Indeed, the cemetery in the center of the city was, just a few short years ago, the magnificent stadium which hosted the Olympics—our universal symbol of peace and harmony.

Bosnia can be that kind of place again. We must not turn our backs on Bosnia now.

A Stand for Freedom Secures America

And so I ask all Americans, and I ask every member of Congress—Democrat and Republican alike—to make the choice for peace. In the choice between peace and war, America must choose peace.

My fellow Americans, I ask you to think just for a moment about this century that is drawing to a close and the new one that will soon begin.

Because previous generations of Americans stood up for freedom and because we continue to do so, the American people are more secure and more prosperous. And all around the world, more people than ever before can hope to build a better life. That is what America's leadership is all about.

We know that these are the blessings of freedom, and America has always been freedom's greatest champion. If we continue to do everything we can to share these blessings with people around the world, if we continue to be leaders for peace, then the next century can be the greatest time our nation has ever known.

A few weeks ago, I was privileged to spend some time with His Holiness Pope John Paul II when he came to America. At the very end of our meeting, the pope looked at me and said, "I have lived through most of this century. I remember that it began with a war in Sarajevo. Mr. President, you must not let it end with a war in Sarajevo."

In Bosnia, this terrible war has challenged our interests and troubled our souls. Thankfully, we can do something about it. I say again, our mission will be clear, limited, and achievable. The people of Bosnia, our NATO allies, and people all around the world are now looking to America for leadership.

So let us lead. That is our responsibility as Americans.

A Leader of Violence in the Balkans Dies Before Being Convicted

Marcus Tanner

The contradictions and conflicts that broke up the country of Yugoslavia were focused most sharply on Bosnia, and at the center of that focus was Serbian leader Slobodan Milosevic. The following viewpoint, written at the time of Milosevic's death, portrays him as both isolated and gregarious, lethal and charming, unscrupulous and devoted, fanatic and uncaring. He directed the suffering and deaths of multitudes and escaped by dying before his international trial concluded. Journalist Marcus Tanner covered the disintegration of the former Yugoslavia for the *Independent* newspaper.

Photo on following page: Former president of Yugoslavia Slobodan Milosevic appears before the International War Crimes Tribunal. (Michel Porro/Getty Images.)

To the end, he cheated his victims. Millions waited years to see Slobodan Milosevic, the so-called Butcher of Belgrade, found guilty for the terror, mass murder and expulsions that Serbian forces visited

SOURCE. Marcus Tanner, "The Bloody Life and Times of the Butcher of Belgrade," *The Independent*, March 12, 2006. www. independent.co.uk. Used by permission of The Independent.

on the unhappy peoples of Yugoslavia in the 1990s. But survivors of the massacres of Vukovar and Srebrenica never got the chance to see his face when a verdict was read out.

His death in a cell at the Scheveningen jail, where he had been a prisoner of the International War Crimes Tribunal since 2001, means that justice never quite got him in the end. Blood pressure and heart trouble got there first.

To those of us who lived in Belgrade at the height of his powers, and who did not share in the then prevailing

A Cherished Croatian City Was an Early Target

While the fighting in Bosnia claimed by far the most lives in the Balkan conflict of the 1990s, the severe violence and destruction began in neighboring Croatia. It included a siege of the beautiful and ancient Croatian coastal city of Dubrovnik.

Croatia declared itself an independent country in June 1991. Right away it enacted laws that targeted Orthodox Serbs. Serb-led forces responded by invading Croatia in July. With superior armaments, they attacked several cities and towns, overwhelming Croatian defenders and drawing little response from the international community.

The shelling of Dubrovnik, from the mountains above it, began in October 1991. It continued despite Serbs and Croats agreeing in December to a US-sponsored cease-fire. Attacks slackened somewhat, but the siege did not end until April 1992. Overall, the shelling killed more than a hundred civilians and damaged 563 of the old city's 824 buildings.

Years later, tourism returned to the rebuilt pearl of the Adriatic Sea, as Dubrovnik has been called, but just inside the main entrance in the massive city wall is a memorial to those who perished. It includes a chart showing where each shell landed.

adulation, he was a terrifying figure. Apparently in absolute control of the passions of almost the entire Serbian nation in the late 1980s and early 1990s, he made use of this morbid skill to send his people off the precipice like lemmings into a series of catastrophic wars with their erstwhile Yugoslav compatriots.

Like Hitler, he seemed to receive much of his strength from the vast, Nuremberg-style rallies that were a hallmark of his early years as Serbian leader. In Kosovo in 1989, at ceremonies marking the 500th anniversary of the historic Battle of Kosovo against the Turks, I watched him sweep out of his limousine. Flanked by prelates of the Serbian Orthodox Church, he addressed the biggest rally of them all in front of about a million adoring Serbs. For me, that day in 1989 provided a rare glimpse of a man who otherwise led a secretive existence in the fortress-like home in the Belgrade suburb of Dedinje with only his deluded termagant of a wife, Mirjana, and two children, Marko and Marija, for company.

> "Milosevic was a brazen, bloody chancer who gambled correctly on the weaknesses besetting the European powers."

From there, after he took power in Serbia in 1987, he plotted one violent adventure after another. There were "only" about 60 Albanian deaths when he sent the Yugoslav army and Serbian police charging into Kosovo to suppress its autonomy in 1989—an action that the other Yugoslav leaders foolishly acquiesced in. Then it was the turn of Croatia, where about 10,000 died in fighting in 1991 after that republic seceded from Yugoslavia.

A Slippery Leader Eluded Opponents

After that, keeping a tally of the figures became useless. In the war that followed in Bosnia in 1992–95, at least 100,000 were killed. Most were Muslims, murdered by well-armed Serb forces in the spring of 1992 as they raced from one undefended town in north and east Bosnia to another, on a mission to drive out Muslims and Croats and so make possible Bosnia's annexation by Serbia. A new phrase entered the lexicon as a result—"ethnic cleansing"—a rough translation of the chilling phrase used by state-run Radio Belgrade.

In retrospect, Milosevic was a brazen, bloody chancer who gambled correctly on the weaknesses besetting the European powers. Time and again, diplomats made their way to Belgrade with their ultimatums, only to leave mollified by Milosevic's expressions of wide-eyed innocence.

As Adam Lebor, author of a book on Milosevic, noted, he had a chameleon-like ability to switch off playing the dictator and turn on a folksy charm. Mr Lebor recalled one British diplomat who left one such encounter not quite persuaded by what he had heard. "Milosevic gave the impression he did not care about people as individuals," he told Mr Lebor. "Nothing seemed to affect him emotionally. Any kind of human suffering just did not register."

Indeed, he even arranged for the murder of the best man at his and Mirjana's wedding, Ivan Stambolic, who was also his predecessor as President of Serbia. Stambolic was kidnapped in 1999 and killed, almost certainly by secret service agents acting on Milosevic's orders.

Or was he? The great problem about establishing Milosevic's responsibility for the carnage of the 1990s was the secretive style, which has made it hard to establish who gave orders. This dilemma has dogged the tribunal prosecutors ever since 2001, when the Serbs, now disillusioned with their former idol, turned him over to the court.

Milosevic soon recovered his equilibrium, hectoring judges and disconcerting witnesses with his mocking and jeering. As the tribunal's former chief prosecutor Richard Goldstone said yesterday [March 11, 2005], he was completely unrepentant. "In spite of his health, he had started to enjoy the trial, and was keen to outwit the tribunal," he said.

Tribunal experts yesterday described his death as a severe blow to international justice. "It's an absolute tragedy that there will now never be a final judgment about

Milosevic," the Balkan expert Tim Judah said. "Without that definitive judgment for future generations, the question of whether he was guilty of genocide will always be disputed now." His death also follows embarrassingly soon after the prison suicide of one of Milosevic's former cronies in Croatia, Milan Babic. "In less than 10 days two important Serbs have died in custody," said Gordana Igric, a London-based Serbian journalist. "Serb nationalists will be asking why they should hand over Ratko Mladic when, as they will say, 'Serbs are dying in The Hague.'"

Even if it is too much to say Milosevic had the last laugh, his death is certainly, as Adam Lebor put it, "very frustrating," as he went to his grave without showing a glimmer of remorse.

Fifteen Years Later, Serbia Condemns a Mass Slaughter

Ron Synovitz

In 1995 Serbs carried out the worst massacre of the conflict in Bosnia, killing eight thousand Muslims in Srebrenica. In 2010 the Serbian parliament apologized for not having done enough to prevent the massacre. The following viewpoint finds that some Serbs are reluctant to acknowledge the slaughter, while others don't think the parliament admitted all that it should have. It is noteworthy that the parliament's resolution does not use the word "genocide." American newspaper and radio journalist Ron Synovitz has worked for Radio Free Europe/Radio Liberty since 1995, reporting from more than twenty countries.

SOURCE. Ron Synovitz, "Serbian Lawmakers Condemn Srebrenica Massacre," Radio Free Europe/Radio Liberty, March 30, 2010. www. rferl.org. Used by permission.

Afer a heated debate, the Serbian parliament has approved a landmark resolution condemning the 1995 Srebrenica massacre of 8,000 Bosnian Muslims, ending years of denial.

The declaration, which condemns the massacre—but stops short of calling it a genocide—and offers an apology to the victims, was adopted with a narrow majority of 127 votes of the 250-seat parliament.

It also stressed the importance of arresting Ratko Mladic, the fugitive general who commanded Bosnian Serb forces at Srebrenica and has been indicted by the UN's war crimes tribunal on charges of genocide.

Ruling coalition member Nenad Canak, leader of the League of Social Democrats, said after the vote that there is still much work for Serbs to do about war crimes that were committed in their name during the 1990s. "The declaration that we just voted on in the Serbian parliament is just the beginning, simply because the subject of this declaration is the tip of the iceberg of the past that we have to confront," Canak said. "This war crime we can't leave to the future generations."

The contentious vote followed a painful reopening of a chapter of Serbia's recent past. Bosnian Serb troops and Serbian paramilitary forces killed some 8,000 Bosnian Muslim men and boys in the UN-protected enclave in July 1995—the worst atrocity in Europe since World War II.

With Serbia seeking to join the European Union, a resolution that took two months to write was proposed to highlight Belgrade's efforts to come to terms with atrocities committed in the name of Serbs during the Balkan wars of the 1990s.

Nada Kolundzija, parliamentary leader of the ruling Democratic Party, told lawmakers during the debate on March 30 [2010] that Belgrade must

> Many Serbs still deny the Srebrenica massacre, despite recognition by the United Nations and the European Union that the killings were an act of genocide.

show the world it has distanced itself from the crimes that were committed during the 1990s. "What we have to do today is say that Serbia does not stand behind those who committed this crime, Serbia does not discriminate between victims, Serbia equally appreciates every victims, expressing, first of all, deep empathy for the victims of others," Kolundzija said.

The Resolution Omits "Genocide"

But many Serbs still deny the Srebrenica massacre, despite recognition by the United Nations and the European Union that the killings were an act of genocide.

The wording of the resolution expresses sympathy for Srebrenica's victims and apologizes for not doing enough to prevent the massacre, but it does not call the killings genocide.

Instead, it condemns "the crime as it is described" in a 2009 European Parliamentary resolution, which—along with a 2007 ruling by the International Court of Justice, uses the word "genocide" to describe the Srebrenica killings.

Radoslav Stojanovic, a professor of international law in Belgrade, tells RFE/RL's [Radio Free Europe/Radio Liberty] Balkan Service that such international resolutions and rulings allow Serbian lawmakers to acknowledge Srebrenica as "genocide" without actually using the word "genocide" themselves.

"Because the International Court of Justice in its ruling of 2007 held that the crimes that took place in Srebrenica were genocide, therefore in our declaration we don't have to worry or to invent a qualification for the crime in Srebrenica," Stojanovic says. "We only need to quote the ruling of the International Court of Justice, in which it is clearly stated that the crime that was committed in Srebrenica was a crime of genocide."

Meho Omerovic, a representative of the Bosniak Sandzak Democratic Party, said it was now vital for

Photo on previous page: A Bosnian Muslim woman sits in front of a wall covered with photos of the victims of the Srebrenica massacre. (AP Photo/ Amel Emric.)

Serbia to capture Mladic—who is suspected of hiding in Serbia—and send him to the UN's war crimes court for trial.

The Truth Is a Sensitive Subject

Jelena Trivan, a member of parliament from President Boris Tadic's Democratic Party, told RFE/RL ahead of the March 30 debate that some Serbs were in denial about the killings at Srebrenica—five years after Tadic himself paid tribute to the victims.

"This is because we live in a country where [even the] broadcasting of a film about Srebrenica in 2005 led to demands for the management of the television station to be punished for showing the truth about Srebrenica," Trivan said. "Because Boris Tadic was almost lynched because he apologized and bowed to the victims of Srebrenica."

In the Republika Srpska, the Bosnian Serb entity of Bosnia-Herzegovina, there is strong opposition to recognizing Srebrenica as genocide or apologizing for the killings there. Many Bosnian Serbs say their community also suffered from war crimes committed by Bosniaks and Bosnian Croats.

Among them is Slavko Jovicic, a member of the Bosnian parliament from the People's Social Democratic Party of Republika Srpska's Prime Minister Milorad Dodik. Jovicic says that the draft resolution actually exacerbates tensions in the Balkans instead of moving the region toward reconciliation.

"I have the right to say openly, on behalf of the victims from my people, that as long as I am here—and I hope other colleagues, too—that this cannot be adopted. That is not possible," Jovicic says. "I know from numerous contacts with voters in Republika Srpska what they have told me. Even if another 15 years pass, maybe another parliament will have more strength and maybe some new truth will come out that will bring our positions closer. I am certain that we will not achieve peace [by adopting this resolution]. We are going toward new conflicts and confrontations of an unforeseeable magnitude."

A Final Step Is Awaited

Meanwhile, even a Serbian apology would be little comfort for Bosnian Muslims like Ilijas Pilav, a Sarajevo surgeon who survived the July 1995 attack by escaping through the woods. Along with thousands of other Muslim men and boys, he had trekked for six days and nights through wilderness before reaching safety.

Pilav told Reuters it was "an experience that no words can describe," one that has left deep traces on his life that "no amount of time and no political declaration can ease."

Pilav said a Serbian parliament resolution that does not call the crime genocide would only add insult to injury.

Janja Bec, a Serbian human rights activist who lectures on genocide at universities, says Belgrade is taking a step forward to even talk about the Srebrenica killings. She says that "denial" is the final stage of genocide. But she also says the failure of the Serbian parliament to use the word "genocide" could inflame tensions in the Balkans.

'This is so insulting that it could badly influence the relations in the region. . . . A crime like this deserves the recognition that it really took place.'

"This is so insulting that it could badly influence the relations in the region," Bec says. "Not only now, but for the next several generations. A crime like this deserves the recognition that it really took place."

The Srebrenica massacre was carried out by Bosnian Serb soldiers and Serbian paramilitaries under the command of Mladic, the Bosnian Serbs' wartime army chief. Mladic is now a fugitive from international law who has been indicted by the UN war crimes tribunal in The Hague on charges of genocide and crimes against humanity.

When Mladic led the Bosnian Serb onslaught against the UN-protected enclave of Srebrenica, he entered the town accompanied by Serbian camera crews, declaring Srebrenica as a "gift to Serbs" and a kind of retaliation for the conquest of Bosnia by the Ottoman Turkish empire.

The European Union has made the capture and extradition of Mladic to The Hague tribunal a condition for progress in Belgrade's accession bid. Many people think he is hiding in Serbia with the help of Belgrade officials.

CHAPTER 2

Controversies Surrounding the Bosnian Conflict

Ethnic Conflict Was Not the Central Cause of the Strife in Bosnia

Susan L. Woodward

Explaining the Bosnian conflict as solely the result of ethnic hatred is to start at the end of the story, the following viewpoint asserts. The author explains that what really caused the turmoil in Bosnia and other parts of the former Yugoslavia was economic and political upheaval. Citizens and institutions in the region were under pressure to abandon socialism and adapt Western Europe's free-market system. In the meantime, the region's political structures were coming apart. Susan L. Woodward is a senior fellow at the Brookings Institution and the author of *Socialist Unemployment: The Political Economy of Yugoslavia, 1945–1990*. In 1994 she served as a senior adviser to the top UN official in the former Yugoslavia.

SOURCE. Susan L. Woodward, "Introduction," *Balkan Tragedy: Chaos and Dissolution After the Cold War*. Washington: The Brookings Institution, 1995, pp. 13–20. Used by permission.

The conflict [in the former Yugoslavia] was simultaneously a matter of domestic transformation and of the transformation of the European and international order. Domestic conflicts became defined in terms of sovereignty and independence, whereas the actions of regional and international institutions were undermining state sovereignty and at the same time so based on unquestioning protection of the principle of sovereignty that they could not address the issue of sovereignty itself. The international prerogative to intervene to protect fundamental human rights appeared to lack both the instruments and the conception of how and when to intervene in circumstances when the process of transforming citizenship rights becomes a matter of national rights, group survival, and incompatible territorial claims. Major powers saw no strategic interest in acting to prevent territorial war, only to find the wars challenging all the premises of their security regimes.

To the extent that the Yugoslav crisis is recognized correctly as an early case of a larger phenomenon that must be addressed, it has been defined as ethnic conflict. Although the major powers attempting to resolve that crisis had fundamental disagreements, they in fact began from the same premise that the conflict was caused by personal hatreds and animosities that they labeled ethnic. The black-and-white portrayal of ethnic conflict that characterized discussion of the Yugoslav case is, in fact, an understandable and potent way to generate sympathy and mobilize loyalties and support for action, particularly when there are clearly innocent victims of armed aggression and when the weaponry of late twentieth-century warfare is so destructive and in abundant supply. This tendency is reinforced by the effects of global interdependence on the formulation of domestic foreign policy. Political and intellectual migration has made ethnic lobbies of émigrés potent single-interest groups in major capitals. The global mass media can

> "The definition of the Yugoslav crisis as ethnic conflict was a major source of the quicksand into which intervention fell."

truly internationalize the tactics of local contests through vivid televised images of human cruelty and through the use of apparently familiar religious, racial, and cultural symbols. The resulting empathy and personal identification are more influential the less governments see a strategic interest to define early action because foreign policy is then more vulnerable to the domestic electoral calculations of governing parties and the political pressures of legislative assemblies.

The definition of the Yugoslav crisis as ethnic conflict was a major source of the quicksand into which intervention fell. Although they were accused of excusing the crimes of nationalist demagogues, those who held the view that this was ethnic conflict and civil war ran into difficulty because they accepted the argument of nationalists, giving credence to the war propaganda of politicians and generals who sought national states and accepted the necessity of war to that end. Those who insisted that this was not civil war but external aggression were drawn increasingly toward the same conclusion— an ethnically defined solution in Bosnia-Herzegovina and in Croatia, because they defined that aggression and its victims ethnically—Serbs against Bosnian Muslims or Croats. But by giving in to an ethnic account of the conflict and defending only one nation in a multinational context, proponents of the aggression theory abandoned the *non*-ethnic understanding and constitutional mechanisms necessary to protect that group (and all citizens in general) against discrimination, expulsion, and death on the basis of their ethnicity/nationality.

That these wars are a form of aggression is indisputable. But the focus on aggression diverts attention from its immediate cause—the breakup of a country and the contest over the location of new frontiers—and from the role that the United States and European powers together played in that process in 1990–92. And while the distinction between external and internal aggression and between aggressive and defensive military action may be the only perch for international actors who seek to hold to international norms those responsible for the atrocities, detention camps, and forced migrations, it is of very little use in influencing behavior when the driving political dynamic is nationalism. In order to combine moral principles with effective policy, the interactive character of competing nationalisms cannot be ignored, and the escalatory spiral of defensive perception and aggressive behavior must be counteracted to stop the violence.

The counterintuitive character of such a dynamic can be seen particularly in the outcome of the argument that such aggression in the Yugoslav case was the plan of one man, Slobodan Milošević. This argument ignores the conditions that make such leaders possible and popular and therefore also ignores the policies necessary to end their rule. It also led people to ascribe so much power to the man that foreign governments came to rely on him to end the wars and therefore could not risk his fall from power even while they accused him of crimes against humanity. Why did Yugoslav society take the turn it did at the end of the 1980s? Why did the economic and political reform of a socialist country bring nationalists to the fore in most of its regions? Why is the dynamic in the former Yugoslavia so similar to that seen elsewhere in the former Soviet Union and in parts of Africa?

> " The real origin of the Yugoslav conflict is the disintegration of governmental authority and the breakdown of a political and civil order. "

Economic Decline Was a Key Factor

The real origin of the Yugoslav conflict is the disintegration of governmental authority and the breakdown of

Peace demonstrators marching towards the parliament building are fired upon by snipers in Sarajevo on April 5, 1992. (AP Photo/ Delich.)

a political and civil order. This process occurred over a prolonged period. The conflict is not a result of historical animosities and it is not a return to the precommunist past; it is the result of the politics of transforming a socialist society to a market economy and democracy. A critical element of this failure was economic decline, caused largely by a program intended to resolve a foreign debt crisis. More than a decade of austerity and declining living standards corroded the social fabric and the rights and securities that individuals and families had come to rely on. Normal political conflicts over economic resources between central and regional governments and over the economic and political reforms of the debt-repayment package became constitutional conflicts and then a crisis of the state itself among politicians who were unwilling to compromise. Such a contest over fundamentally different views of the role of government and its economic powers would be fought between competing political parties in parliamentary and democratic regimes. But in this transitional, one-party, but highly decentralized federation, the contestants were government leaders fighting to retain or enhance their political jurisdictions and public property rights over economic resources within their territories. The more they quarreled, the more they contributed to the incapacity and declining authority of the central government to regulate and to resolve those conflicts over economic rights and political powers of subordinate governments.

This story would be incomplete and might easily have had a quite different outcome, however, if the internal events had not been accompanied by a disintegration of the international order in which the country found its place. As is characteristic of small states, the domestic order of socialist Yugoslavia was strongly influenced by its place in the international order: its geopolitical location, its patterns of trade and foreign alliances, and the requirements of participation in the international economy and its various organizations. The viability of the Yugoslav regime, in fact, depended on its foreign position and a policy of national independence and non-alignment tied to the organization of the cold war world. By the 1960s that viability had also come to depend on access to foreign credits and capital markets on the basis of Yugoslavia's strategic position in the Balkans and its independent foreign policy. The process that brought the cold war to an end challenged and undermined that strategic significance, the role of the Yugoslav army, and the country's alternative markets in the East and in the third world without providing any new bases for security and domestic political and economic viability.

In the collapse of Yugoslavia the link between these two processes, the domestic and the international, is the state. The global campaign of major powers and financiers during the 1980s to promote economic liberalization had as a premise the idea that states had taken on too much control in managing their economies during the stagflationary conditions of the world economy during the 1970s. Economic revival required liberalization, privatization, and cuts in public expenditures for welfare, public employment, and social services. At the same time anticommunists within communist-ruled countries and in the West were declaring the problem of socialism to be the power of their states—so-called totalitarian control and overweening bureaucracies. The West's euphoria over the collapse of communist states and its insistence on market reform, privatization, and slashed budgets as conditions for economic aid and trade paid little regard to the alternative hypotheses—that the crisis of these countries grew from governments that were too weak; that to achieve the prescribed reforms required an extremely effective administrative capacity; that foreign creditors will lend only to governments that guarantee repayment; and that foreign investors demand favorable governmental regulations and political stability.

The more unstable an international order, the more governments must resume responsibility for external defense and for negotiating foreign trade and the conditions for it on which all modern economies depend. Radical reorientation to market demand of exports and production cannot occur without new investment

> Economic reforms such as those demanded of Yugoslavia . . . ask for political suicide.

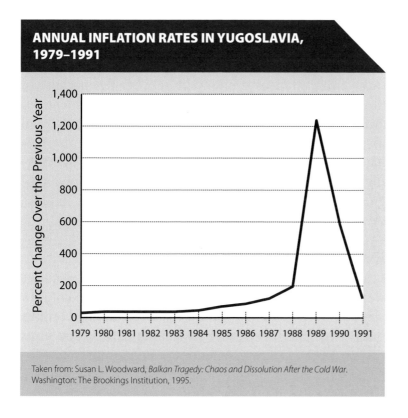

ANNUAL INFLATION RATES IN YUGOSLAVIA, 1979–1991

Taken from: Susan L. Woodward, *Balkan Tragedy: Chaos and Dissolution After the Cold War.* Washington: The Brookings Institution, 1995.

for structural adjustments, and successful open-market economies require a centralized capacity for macroeconomic policy. Entrepreneurship and civil freedoms depend on a context of civil order, predictability, and individual security.

Economic reforms such as those demanded of Yugoslavia by foreign creditors and Western governments ask for political suicide: they require governments to reduce their own powers. They also do so at the same time that the demands on governments, particularly the necessity to protect civil order and to provide stability in the midst of rapid change, are ever greater. Without a stable civil and legal order, the social conditions that are created can be explosive: large-scale unemployment among young people and unskilled urban dwellers; demobilized soldiers and security police looking for private employment; thriving conditions for black market activities and crime; and nourishing local and global traffic in small arms and ammunition. A sense of community under these circumstances is highly prized, but not because of the historical persistence and power of ethnic identities and cultural attachments, as the ethnic conflict school insists, but because the bases of existing communities have collapsed and governments are radically narrowing what they will or can provide in terms of previously guaranteed rights to subsistence, land, public employment, and even citizenship. . . .

Events Outpaced Politicians

Less than six months after the first democratic elections were held in the former Yugoslav republics, the country was at war. In July 1991, three weeks after war had broken out between an independence-seeking Croatia and units of the Yugoslav army defending the country's territorial integrity and, in some localities, Serbs who opposed Croatia's secession, top-level political advisers in Zagreb and Belgrade insisted that a political solution would still be found. While barricades were being erected in the city of Mostar in Bosnia-Herzegovina and the main transport link between Bosnia and Croatia—the bridge at Bosanski Šamac—was being blown up on February 5, 1992, the Bosnian government was still preparing a referendum on independence, and all of Sarajevo was convinced it would be spared war. Two months later the more than two-year-long siege of Sarajevo by Bosnian Serb artillery fire began. In the summer of 1993, three weeks before the central Bosnian town of Vitez was nearly leveled by bombs and fire and its Muslim citizens massacred by Bosnian Croats, a high-level delegation visiting from a Western defense ministry insisted that Vitez was calm and safe from war.

Unprepared for the rapidity of the political changes, inexperienced in creating new governments, and preoccupied with revolution against the previous regime and their own ambitions, the politicians who emerged in this rapidly changing scene were neither predisposed nor well prepared to develop the guarantees and procedures for human rights and free debate and to accept the compromises and temporary defeats necessary to stable, pluralistic democracies. A top adviser to Russian president Boris Yeltsin [Sergei Stankevich] characterized the general problem in August 1992: "The most important thing to know about the Russian democrats and Yeltsin is that power came to us unexpectedly." Under these circumstances, the positive assistance, or absence of negative influence, from major powers and international organizations takes on critical importance.

> Ethnic differences, even substantial differences, do not set a society inexorably on a path toward war.

Already deep Western involvement in Yugoslavia shifted belatedly to explicit intervention to try to save the country or to mediate its dissolution only when nationalist and autonomist goals had taken over. Understanding little about the concept of national self-determination and the consequence of pursuing national states in a multinational setting, external actors did little to counteract the escalating momentum of confrontation and violence and did much to make matters worse.

Ethnic differences, even substantial differences, do not set a society inexorably on a path toward war. Few states are free of the potential for animosity along ethnic, religious, racial, or communal lines. All countries have histories, even unresolved quarrels and unexpunged traumas, but they do not inevitably become the cause of war. In societies like the United States, ethnic differences are valued for enhancing the quality of life through variety and creative tension, even if ethnic conflicts also arise. Tensions along ethnic, racial, or historical fault lines can lead to civil violence, but to explain the Yugo-slav crisis as a result of ethnic hatred is to turn the story upside down and begin at its end. . . .

Western Leaders Were Biased

The war in Bosnia and Herzegovina did eventually evoke pity for Muslim victims and for the people of Sarajevo, leading to the largest UN operation ever to deliver humanitarian relief and protect relief workers. But this operation was part of a policy that aimed to do everything possible to avoid military involvement in support of a particular political objective. Instead, outsiders insisted that the Yugoslavs were not like them, that such atrocities always characterized the troublesome region and its penchant for war and balkanization, that more than anything else the violence demonstrated the difference between *them* and *us*. Continuing to view the conflict as irrelevant to their national interests and collective security, Western leaders defined it as anachronistic, an unpleasant reminder of old ethnic and religious conflicts that modern Europe had left behind, rather than as part of their own national competition to redefine Europe and respond to the end of the cold war. Even the morally outraged used a language of distinctions in their label of barbarism: the "otherness" of nations capable of such evil. This act of dismissal—itself profoundly nationalist in its core sentiment of prejudicial exclusion of whole peoples defined by their origin as different, even subhuman, and thus of little consequence—justified inaction. It was thus for most surviving Yugoslavs the greater tragedy of the wars.

Religion Was the Main Issue Behind the Attacks in Bosnia

Michael A. Sells

The following viewpoint explains that, whether defined as Serbs, Croatians, or Bosnians, the people of the Balkans had lived together for five centuries with a common language and heritage. Their religions differed, yet all faiths were tolerated—until Serb and Croat extremists decided to wipe out all traces of non-Christian worship, history, and culture, the author states. Their special targets were mosques, museums, and libraries, in an attempt to erase a multireligious culture. The author asserts that the term "ethnic cleansing" is misleading; the brutal persecution of Muslims in particular was based on religious identity. Michael A. Sells is a professor of Islamic history and literature in the Divinity School of the University of Chicago. He has written and edited numerous books.

SOURCE. Michael A. Sells, "Fire in the Pages," *The Bridge Betrayed: Religion and Genocide in Bosnia*. Berkeley, Los Angeles, and London: University of California Press, 1996, pp. 1–15. Used by permission.

"It was the most apocalyptic thing I'd ever seen," said Aida Mušanović, an artist from Sarajevo, describing the burning of the National Library in Sarajevo. For days, a thick black cloud of ash hung over the city and residents would find pieces of charred paper or ashes of burned books and manuscripts in their hair and on their clothes.

On August 25, 1992, the Serb army began shelling the National Library of Bosnia-Herzegovina in Sarajevo from positions on the mountainside directly in front of it. In the next few days, in the largest book-burning in modern human history, over a million books, more than a hundred thousand manuscripts and rare books, and centuries of historical records of Bosnia-Herzegovina went up in flames. Volunteers formed a human chain to rescue what they could. One of them, a graduate student at the University of Sarajevo, never made it home.

> The destruction of the National Library was one component of a systematic campaign of cultural eradication.

What was in the pages of those manuscripts and rare books, survivors of centuries of peace and war, that the Serb army was determined to destroy? What was there in those burning pages that many Sarajevans—Croats, Serbs, Muslims, and Jews—were willing to risk their lives to save?

The destruction of the National Library was one component of a systematic campaign of cultural eradication. Three months earlier, on May 17, 1992, the Serb army had targeted the Oriental Institute in Sarajevo, which housed the largest collection of Islamic and Jewish manuscripts in southeast Europe. More than five thousand manuscripts in Hebrew, Persian, Arabic, Turkish, and Adzămijski (Slavic in Arabic script) were incinerated.

The Serb army then turned its fire on the National Museum, hitting it repeatedly and destroying much of its contents. One special item was saved: an ancient Jewish prayer book used for celebration of the *seder* or Passover feast. The *Sarajevo Haggadah*, with its exquisite Hebrew calligraphy and colored illustration, had been created in fourteenth-century Spain. Jewish refugees from the Inquisition in Spain had brought it to Bosnia. During World War II the *Sarajevo Haggadah* had been preserved by a Muslim curator who hid it from Nazi soldiers. In 1992, it was saved at great personal risk by a team of Bosnian museum workers that included a Muslim, an Orthodox Serb, and a Catholic. The *Haggadah* has thus survived three historic persecutions: the expulsion of the Jews from Spain in 1492, the Holocaust, and what has been called "ethnic cleansing" in Bosnia.

The shelling of these cultural institutions was purposeful. They were chosen for destruction and shelled in a precise manner. Areas around them were left untouched. During one particular shelling of the National Museum, the Serb gunners missed and struck the Holiday Inn directly in front of it. Kate Adie, a BBC reporter, interviewed the Serb officer afterward. When she asked him why he had been shelling the Holiday Inn, the major hotel for journalists in Sarajevo, the officer apologized, explaining that he had been aiming at the museum and had struck the Holiday Inn by mistake.

Interreligious Life and Institutions Attacked

Since April 1992 the Serb army has targeted for destruction the major libraries, manuscript collections, museums, and other cultural institutions in Sarajevo, Mostar, and other besieged cities. What the Serb artillery missed, the Croat nationalist militia known as the "Croatian Defense Council" (HVO) took care of.

Where the Serb and Croat armies have been able to get closer than shelling range, the destruction has been even greater. The Croatian Defense Council dynamited mosques

> "The Croat and Serb nationalists have destroyed an estimated fourteen hundred mosques. . . . Every evidence of their existence has been effaced."

and Orthodox churches throughout the regions controlled by the Croat military. Serb militias have dynamited all the mosques (over six hundred) in areas they have occupied, some of them masterworks of European architecture such as the sixteenth-century Ferhadija Mosque in Banja Luka and the Colored Mosque in Foča built in 1551. Between them, the Croat and Serb nationalists have destroyed an estimated fourteen hundred mosques. In many cases the mosques have been ploughed over and turned into parking lots or parks; every evidence of their existence has been effaced. Graveyards, birth records, work records, and other traces of the Bosnian Muslim people have been eradicated.

Western political leaders have spoken of "ancient animosities," portraying Bosnians as a group of Balkan tribal killers who have hated one another for centuries and who are incapable of living in peace. In the fires of the National Library, the irony of that portrayal becomes apparent. What the Serb and Croat armies were destroying, there and elsewhere, was the graphic and palpable evidence of over five hundred years of interreligious life in Bosnia. Despite the wars and strife of the past, religious monuments and houses of worship in Mostar and Sarajevo had been built next to one another and shared the same skyline. It is this architectural, literary, and human evidence—the monuments, the books, and the people who treasured them—of a flourishing multi-confessional culture that ethnoreligious militants have sought to efface.

History Rewritten Through Violence

The northeast Bosnian town of Zvornik was known for its heritage of Bosnian Muslim poets, saints, rebels, and mystics. From April through July of 1992 the Serb military killed or expelled the entire Muslim population. After all the mosques in the primarily Muslim town were dynamited and ploughed over, the new Serb nationalist mayor declared: "There never were any mosques in Zvornik." Destroyed with those mosques was the evidence not only of the Muslim heritage of Zvornik but also of five hundred years of shared living between Christians and Muslims. History could now be rewritten according to the desires of those who wished to claim that this land was always and purely Christian Serb. In May 1993 to celebrate Zvornik's new status as 100 percent "pure" and cleansed of all Muslims, the mayor dedicated a new church, renamed a local, formerly Muslim village "Saint Stephen," and kissed a crucifix.

Aida Mušanović, the artist who described the burning of the National Library, had visited the hospital in Sarajevo and seen the carnage brought by the war. Yet the burning of the library struck her with a special horror. In the fire of the National Library, she realized that what she was experiencing was not only war but also something else. The centuries of culture that fell back in ash onto the besieged city revealed a secret. The gunners on the hills above Sarajevo did not seek to defeat an enemy army; at that time, there was no organized, opposing army. They sought to take territory, but not only territory. They sought political concessions, but also something more. Their goal was the eradication of a people and all evidence of that people's culture and existence. . . .

Bosnian Enemies Share Ethnicity and Language

The word "ethnic" in "ethnic cleansing" is a euphemism. Bosnian Serbs, Croats, and Muslims all speak the same language, despite the fact that for political reasons they each call it now by a different name. They all trace their descent to tribes that migrated to the area around the sixth century and were Slavic in language and culture by the time they settled in the area. Those who have been singled out for persecution have fallen on the wrong side of a dividing line based solely on religious identity.

As in most wars, innocent civilians from all sides have suffered in the war, the quest for territory, and population expulsions. But Bosnian Muslims—and those who would share a body-politic with them—have been the victims of a consistently more brutal and more methodical violence. Even in the context of the conflict between Croatian and Serb nationalists, who engage in expulsions and atrocities against each other's population as a continuation of the conflict of World War II, the Muslim population has been separated out and treated (by both Croat and Serb nationalists) with particular cruelty. Most victims were Bosnian Muslim noncombatants in areas taken by Serb and Croat militias without significant combat.

In such cases, Muslim religious identity was determined by strictly extrinsic criteria. A Bosnian Muslim in a Serb or Croat camp was there not because of any particular act, expression, or thought. Some in the targeted population defined themselves as Muslims according to the Islamic testimony of belief in one deity and in Muhammad as the messenger of the one deity. Some were observant, for example, keeping the required fast during the Islamic holy month of Ramadan or the prohibition against pork and alcohol. Some were unobservant. Many Bosnian Muslims were atheists. Many were observant of some of the Islamic practices such as the Ramadan fast but considered themselves religious skeptics and their observances cultural. Some supported the political leaders of the Bosnian government; some did not. Some were indifferent to politics.

In the 1971 census a new national category of "Muslims" in Bosnia was recognized by the Yugoslav govern-

ment. This nationality label led to numerous contradictions within Yugoslavia: an Albanian Muslim was not considered to be a "Muslim" in the Yugoslav census of nationalities, but many Bosnians of Muslim background who considered themselves atheists or skeptics declared themselves "Muslim" in the census to avoid the categories of "Serb" and "Croat," both of which had religious implications. For those who wanted a Bosnian nationality to be affirmed, alongside those of Croat, Slovene, Macedonian, Serbian, and Albanian, this classification of "Muslim" was problematic; it finally gave Bosnian Muslims a political voice alongside Catholics and Orthodox Serbs, but it did so at the cost of further reinforcing the identity between religion and nationality.

In the world of Omarska [a concentration camp], if an inhabitant of Bosnia had a name identifiable as Muslim or parents with names identifiable as Muslim, that was considered guilt enough, whatever the beliefs

A destroyed mosque in the Muslim village of Ahmici, Croatia. The Serb army targeted mosques as part of their ethnic cleansing campaign. (AP Photo/ David Brauchli.)

or practices of that individual and whether or not that person was categorized as "Muslim" in the nationalities census. Those organizing the persecution, on the other hand, identified themselves and their cause through explicit religious symbols. The symbols appeared in the three-fingered hand gestures representing the Christian trinity, in the images of sacred figures of Serbian religious mythology on their uniform insignia, in the songs they memorized and forced their victims to sing, on the priest's ring they kissed before and after their acts of persecution, and in the formal religious ceremonies that marked the purification of a town of its Muslim population. The term "ethnic" in the expression "ethnic cleansing," then, is a euphemism for "religious." It entails a purely extrinsic yet deadly definition of the victim in terms of religious identity; the intrinsic aspect—in the form of religious mythology—becomes the motivation and justification for atrocities on the part of the perpetrator.

> The term 'ethnic' in the expression 'ethnic cleansing' . . . is a euphemism for 'religious.'

The United States and Western Europe Mishandled the Outbreaks of Violence in Bosnia

Lester H. Brune

During the late 1980s and early 1990s, US presidents decided that whatever problems there were in Yugoslavia were up to Europeans to solve. But European leaders did not act knowledgeably or effectively, according to the following viewpoint. All the major powers that could have prevented violence in the region instead allowed it to happen and, in some ways, made matters worse, the author asserts. Belatedly, US and European diplomats and negotiators became involved, but they underestimated the fervor of potential aggressors. Lester H. Brune is professor emeritus of history at Bradley University and an author on international topics.

SOURCE. Lester H. Brune, "U.S. and Bosnia: Delayed Intervention," *The United States & the Balkan Crisis, 1990–2005: Conflict in Bosnia and Kosovo*. Claremont, CA: Regina Books, 2005, pp. 17–26. Reproduced by permission.

George H.W. Bush's administration decided in 1989 that Yugoslavia had become less vital to the U.S.'s national interest because the Cold War was waning. Thus when disputes began between Yugoslavia's federal government and its three largest republics, Washington policy makers focused on events in Moscow and expected the European Union (EU) to resolve Yugoslavia's difficulties. Unfortunately, the EU did not have the political-military institutions to handle such a crisis.

Although Americans celebrated the end of Soviet communism, the post-Cold War world still needed U.S. leadership to maintain global security, foster democracy and expand free trade. After 1989, Bush thought EU leaders should take charge of European affairs and some EU members welcomed this new stance as a "new age of Europe" independent of U.S. direction. They believed, falsely as it turned out, that mediation between Yugoslav parties would quickly end the fighting.

Both the EU and UN secured numerous cease-fires that were subsequently violated but, because they lacked the ability to enforce them, the fighting spread from Slovenia to Croatia and Bosnia. The results were not only mounting bloodshed, but increased "ethnic cleansings" that ravaged conquered populations in a manner reminiscent of the Nazi holocaust.

Although war crime reports in the Balkans suggested a moral imperative for U.S. intervention, initially President Bush, and later President Clinton, tolerated the atrocities because no vital U.S. national interest was deemed to be present. Reluctantly, but gradually in 1994–1995, Clinton employed the necessary force and persuasion to compel the warring factions to adopt peace accords and committed U.S., European, and Russian forces to implement their terms. For four years, however, the errors and missed opportunities of the EU, UN, and U.S. provided examples of what interventions should and should not attempt.

US Policies Worsened the Conditions in the Region

Yugoslavia's problems that began during Ronald Reagan's presidency reached a serious stage when George Bush entered office. During the Reagan era, [Yugoslav president Josip Broz] Tito's death, the growing tensions in Yugoslavia, and the rise of Serbian and Croatian nationalism were largely ignored. Nevertheless, as [author and former adviser to a top UN official in Yugoslavia] Susan Woodward indicates, Reagan's refusal to condemn human rights violations and willingness to accept "authoritarian" anticommunist regimes provided the breeding ground for authoritarian-nationalistic regimes such as [Slobodan] Milosevic's Serbian Republic and [Franjo] Tudjman's Croatian Republic. In addition, Reagan's economic policies acerbated Yugoslavia's difficulties because he stopped aid to Yugoslavia in 1981 and encouraged World Bank-International Monetary Fund (INF) and the U.S. Agency for International Development (USAID) to allocate loans to Yugoslavia only if it adopted austerity programs that unfortunately stimulated separatist ambitions.

In 1989, Bush appointed Warren Zimmermann as ambassador to Yugoslavia and, judging by Zimmermann's memoirs, neither he nor Assistant Secretary of State Lawrence Eagleburger comprehended the severity of Yugoslavia's problems until early 1990. Both Zimmermann and Eagleburger had earlier served in Yugoslavia, but they would misjudge the intentions of Serbia's Milosevic, whom they had known as a leading economist.

> [US ambassador to Yugoslavia Warren] Zimmermann was surprised at the intensity of Serb nationalism.

Before Zimmermann left for Yugoslavia in March 1989, he and Eagleburger agreed to the change in previous U.S. policy that ended Yugoslavia's status as vital to

Secretary of State James Baker's visit to Belgrade in June 1991 was not enough to convince the Bush administration that US troops should be sent to the region. (AP Photo/John Duricka.)

the U.S.'s national interests because it no longer served as the vital geopolitical crossroad linking Western Europe with Greece and Turkey. Moreover, unlike Poland and Hungary where democracy had begun to flourish, Yugoslavia had been committing human rights violations against Albanians in Kosovo.

Upon arriving in Yugoslavia, Zimmermann was surprised at the intensity of Serb nationalism but initially did not consider this relevant. He found that Milosevic's "trampling on Albanian rights was almost universally popular among Serbs." He met an art historian, a "sensitive woman" who had lived in New York, who said solving Kosovo's problem was "simple, just line all the Albanians up against a wall and shoot them."

The United States Fails to Act Decisively

The decision that Yugoslavia was not important to U.S. national interests limited Washington's backing for Yugoslavia's federal government at a critical time. In April 1989, Zimmermann realized that Prime Minister [Ante] Markovic needed support to reform Yugoslavia's political and economic system but did not fully appreciate the dangers to Markovic's program from leaders of Serbia, Croatia and Slovenia. Markovic had Yugoslavia's Assembly carry out "structural adjustments" of the economy required by the World Bank-IMF, but unemployment and cuts in welfare that followed persuaded many workers that the nationalist measures of Milosevic, [Slovenian leader Milan] Kuchan, and Tudjman would help them more.

> 'I don't want to send young [American] men into a war where I can't see that we are going to prevail.'

To promote Markovic, Zimmermann arranged for him to visit the U.S. in October 1989, but unfortunately the journey simply underscored Americans' inability to understand Yugoslavia's discontent. Markovic's New York discussions with bankers and businessmen provided no economic investments to aid his government and, at the White House, Bush wasted Markovic's time by asking him about Mikhail Gorbachev's Soviet policies and showing no interest in Balkan problems. By December 1989, Zimmermann finally grasped Markovic's problems when Slovenia prohibited Serbs from staging anti-Albanian demonstrations in Ljubljana and Milosevic retaliated by embargoing Serbian trade and finance transactions with Slovenia. After Croatian leaders sided with Slovenia, Markovic could no longer restrain the leaders of these three dominant republics.

Hoping to assist Markovic, Zimmermann persuaded Eagleburger to visit Belgrade in February 1990. In meetings with Markovic and leaders of the various republics, Eagleburger's efforts to convince Milosevic, Tudjman, and Kuchan that their best interests required Yugoslav unity failed. Because of Bush's passive policies, Eagleburger offered Yugoslav leaders nothing except statements in favor of Yugoslav unity—no economic, political or military incentives to change their behavior.

Eagleburger and Zimmermann agreed that Yugoslavia's menacing situation was a European problem and that the U.S. should urge the Europeans to help Markovic. Upon returning to Washington, Eagleburger requested all U.S. embassies to ask the European states to assist Markovic, but this too failed to produce satisfactory results.

Perhaps the underlying reason Bush desired to have the Europeans deal with the Yugoslav problem was his belief that U.S. intervention would pose a serious dilemma. In January 1992, Bush told an interviewer that "I don't want to send young men into a war where I can't see that we are going to prevail and prevail quickly"—a comment *Washington Post* columnist Jim Hoagland promptly dubbed the "Bush doctrine."

Europe Also Had Other Priorities

Of course, European leaders share in the blame for failing to prevent Yugoslavia's break-up and the subsequent bloodshed. Europeans eager to displace American supervision had made some successful steps toward Europe's economic unity; but the EU had not achieved real political or military unification. Neither the European Parlia-

Reporters Revealed Massacres

The reluctance of the United States and Western European nations to become involved in Bosnia diminished after courageous journalists uncovered and reported on the conflict's atrocities. Foremost among those reporters was Roy Gutman of the newspaper *Newsday*.

Gutman's August 2, 1992, dispatch first revealed the extent of torture and slaughter going on in Serb-run death camps. He and journalists such as John Burns of the *New York Times* and Ed Vulliamy of the Guardian informed the world of the extent of the mass rapes and other lethal cruelty, and led to the liberation of captured civilians.

"Roy Gutman freed at least 6,000 men who would still be in detention today," a UN spokeswoman said at the time. In 2010, Gutman was declared an honorary citizen of Sarajevo, Bosnia's capital city.

Some critics accused the news media of taking sides in the Bosnian conflict. In response, Christiane Amanpour, who reported from combat zones for CNN, wrote in *The Quill* in April 1996: "The very notion of objectivity in war becomes immensely important. What does that word mean? I have come to believe that objectivity means giving all sides a fair hearing, but not treating all sides equally."

ment nor the three rotating heads of the European presidency had effective authority, while the European Council of Ministers represented the divergent national interests of Britain, France, Germany, and Italy, not "European" interests. . . .

While the European governments failed to help Markovic keep the Yugoslavia federation together, Zimmermann and Bush had to deal with well-intended but narrowly conceived congressional interference that weakened the already inadequate U.S. backing for Markovic. Influenced by Albanian-American and Croatian-American lobbyists, Congress held hearings on the mistreatment of Albanians in Kosovo. Republicans led by Senators Robert Dole and Alfonse D'Amato and Representative Don Nickles and Democrats led by Representatives Joe Dioguardi and Tom Lantos apparently had little understanding of Yugoslavian political affairs. They could not grasp that Markovic was unable to control the Serb Republic's use of terrorist methods against Albanians in Kosovo.

After visiting Yugoslavia, Dole, D'Amato and Nickles persuaded Congress to pass the Nickles Amendment in November 1990 that would cut off U.S. aid of $5 million to Markovic's government on May 1, 1991, if Yugoslavia did not stop the repression in Kosovo. President Bush opposed the measure but failed to convince Dole to drop the idea because it satisfied Albanian and Croatian lobbyists. The Nickles amendment passed at the time when both Zimmermann and the Central Intelligence Agency (CIA) warned the White House that Markovic's government was faltering. Zimmermann reported that if Slovenia and Croatia seceded, the other republics would be at the "mercies of Serbia" and Bosnia "would make democracy the first casualty." Only U.S. action, he said, might prevent violence and assist Yugoslavian unity. A more pessimistic CIA report anticipated that Milosevic would try to block the secession of Slovenia and Croatia by unleashing civil war and ethnic violence throughout Yugoslavia. The CIA concluded that neither the U.S. nor Europeans could save Yugoslavian unity.

> "The CIA concluded that neither the U.S. nor Europeans could save Yugoslavian unity."

As the June 1991 date for the secession of Slovenia and Croatia approached, the EU and the U.S. undertook last minute steps to preserve Yugoslavia's unity. In March, Markovic asked EU President Jacques Delors for assistance, but EU members sent mixed messages to Belgrade. The EU Parliament responded with a resolution favoring the right of republics to secede if they did so peacefully. However, it also approved Delors' proposal for $4.5 billion economic aid to Yugoslavia if the government protected minority rights and reduced its military and social welfare budgets—policies that had already exacerbated Markovic's difficulties.

The EU's inadequate assistance was followed by an equally ineffective U.S. effort when Secretary of State James Baker visited Belgrade on June 21, 1991. Baker had kept the Nickles Amendment from taking effect and, before arriving, he had attended a meeting of the CSCE [Conference on Security and Cooperation in Europe] that voted to support Yugoslav unity but offered no aid to Markovic. Baker met with Milosevic, Tudjman, Kuchan, [Bosnian president Alija] Izetbegovic, and [Macedonian president Kiro] Gligorov, but found that reason alone was insufficient to unite the interests of the Serbians, Slovenians, and Croatians. The lack of U.S. and European action, however, was taken as a virtual "green light" by Milosevic, Kuchan, and Tudjman to break-up the Federation. Zimmermann called the U.S. and European failure the "paradox of prevention" since they could not obtain the necessary domestic support to prevent Yugoslavia's demise because "circumstances that unambiguously justify such action have not yet arrived."

Shortly after Baker's visit, Slovenia and Croatia declared their independence, throwing Yugoslavia into turmoil. EU and CSCE officials had no plan for dealing with the secession crisis. Both British Foreign Minister Douglas Hurd and U.S. Assistant Secretary of State Eagleburger restated support for Yugoslav unity, but neither government would commit their forces or NATO to insist on a Yugoslav settlement. EU and CSCE representatives gained a cease-fire agreement on July 7, but shortly afterwards fighting broke-out between Croatia and Serbia.

European Efforts Prove Futile

President Bush's decision to let Europeans deal with Yugoslavia's crisis dominated U.S. policy during the next eighteen months. Bush, Secretary Baker and Chairman of the Joint Chiefs General Colin Powell refused to involve American troops to stop the Serb-Croat conflict or to take strong action in April 1992 when fighting began in Bosnia. The State Department only supported the attempts of the EU and CSCE to gain a cease-fire. The reasons for U.S. passivity were several: the claim that Balkan conflicts were inevitable, the lingering "Vietnam Syndrome" that interventions will escalate, Powell's contention that any U.S. military intervention must result in a quick, decisive victory with few casualties, U.S. budget problems, and concern that military intervention would hurt Bush's presidential chances in the 1992 election.

The White House may have possibly desired to test the Europeans' ability to act alone in the post-Cold War world. European leaders such as Luxembourg's Jacques Poos had asserted: "This is the hour of Europe. It is not the hour of America." Together with Italy's Gianni De-Michelis and the Netherlands' Hans van den Broek, Poos thought negotiating a cease-fire between Serbia, Slovenia, and Croatia would be easy. While EU-CSCE mediators strove to maintain the Federation, in reality they negotiated cease-fire terms that weakened Markovic's government, virtually approved Slovenia's independence and resulted in the Serb-Croat war.

Slovenian officials were prepared to secede. The minister of defense, Janez Jansa, had illegally purchased military equipment for its Territorial Defense Force (TDF) and recruited Slovenians from the Yugoslavian National Army (YNA) to assist the secession. After declaring independence, Jansa's TDF and YNA recruits took control of Slovenia's border control posts and customs houses and sought support from the Austrian and German governments.

In contrast to Slovenia's preparedness, Markovic and the federal parliament argued about responding to secession before parliamentary leaders sent the YNA to attack Slovenia and regain control of the borders to Italy and Austria. In two days' fighting, Slovenian forces had prevailed. The YNA suffered 37 deaths, while the Slovenians endured 14 deaths but captured 3,200 YNA prisoners.

In Croatia there were skirmishes between Tudjman's TDF and Croatian Serbs. Their fighting escalated in mid-July when Milosevic's Serb Republic and the YNA ignored the EU-CSCE's July 7 cease-fire and joined the Croatian Serbs to fight for a Greater Serbia. Knowingly or not, EU-CSCE mediators had treated Croatia and Slovenia as sovereign states equal to Markovic's government, not as revolutionaries violating the Yugoslav Constitution. The EU-CSCE claimed to support Markovic but did not differentiate between the Federation and the separatists who were using military force to achieve independence.

Milosevic did not contest Slovenia's secession but rushed armies to help Croatian Serbs in the Krajina, in Eastern Slavonia and along the Dalmatian Coast. As Tudjman vowed continued resistance to Serbian ambitions and built up his military forces, the Serb-Croat conflict became a fierce, bloody war that saw initially victorious Serbs begin an "ethnic cleansing" program.

Poos and EU mediators could not resolve Yugoslavia's problems and, at the suggestion of France, they asked the UN to join peacemaking efforts. Moreover, the European-sponsored July cease-fire actually speeded up Yugoslavia's disintegration in part because the EU usually ignored Markovic and Yugoslav moderates, such as the presidents of Bosnia and Macedonia who wanted unity, and consequently Markovic would resign in December 1991.

A Cease-Fire Prevails Temporarily

The UN levied an arms embargo on all Yugoslavia in September 1991, and UN Secretary General [Boutros] Boutros-Ghali appointed American Cyrus Vance to head mediations in Geneva while Lord Carrington of Britain led EU negotiations at The Hague. Vance concentrated on getting a Serb-Croat cease-fire while Carrington mediated terms for a settlement covering all Yugoslav republics. During these months, Milosevic's Serbs and Croatian Serbs conquered the Krajina of Croatia and most of East Slavonia before besieging the Dalmatian city of Dubrovnik. On November 23, Croatia's Tudjman and Serbia's Milosevic signed Vance's cease-fire proposal. Four days later, the UNSC [UN Security Council] assisted the agreement by approving the deployment of a United Nations Protection Force (UNPROFOR) to separate Serb and Croat armies and monitor the cease-fire. On January 2, 1992, fighting ended when the Serb and Croat military leaders finalized cease-fire zones, and in March, 14,000 UNPROFOR soldiers—most of them from France and Britain but none, of course, from the United States—reached Croatia. . . .

> The EU recognition of Croatia was badly timed . . . [and] left the negotiators without incentives to reach a broad peace agreement.

On December 17 [1991], the EU voted to recognize independence for Slovenia and Croatia on January 15, 1992, and other former Yugoslav republics which met the stated standards on human rights, disarmament, and regional security.

The EU recognition of Croatia was badly timed, coming when the Vance Plan prepared the cease-fire between Serbs and Croats and the UNPROFOR mission prepared to monitor the Croat-Serb cease-fire. The EU ignored Carrington and Vance, who protested that recognition left the negotiators without incentives to reach a broad peace agreement for all Yugoslav republics.

The EU's resolution convinced Bosnian leaders to plan for immediate independence. Although President Izetbegovic was preparing a February 1992 referendum on independence, he was challenged on January 9, when Bosnian Serbs declared independence for their Republic of Srpska. This declaration prompted EU President Jose Cutileiro to propose negotiations at Lisbon on a plan for a confederation government along Serb, Muslim, and Croat ethnic-cultural lines in Bosnia. Neither the Bosnian Muslims nor the Bosnian Serbs liked the plan, but Ambassador Zimmermann indicated that the Bosnian Serbs would accept it if they could have two-thirds of Bosnian territory, an idea which neither Izetbegovic nor Cutileiro accepted.

The Bosnian government held its plebiscite on independence on February 29 and March 1, but the Bosnian Serbs boycotted it. Without Serb participation, two-thirds of Bosnia's total population voted and a majority of 99 percent approved independence. On April 5–6, the EU and the U.S. recognized the Republic of Bosnia-Herzegovina but ignored [Radovan] Karadzic's claim to an independent Republic of Srpska.

When Bosnia was recognized on April 5, war had already begun because Bosnian Serb paramilitary, assisted by Milosevic's YNA, attacked Muslim and Croat villages. Using the YNA's heavy weapons, Serb artillery bombarded Sarajevo in early April and a conflict ensued which resulted in atrocities committed by both participants but mostly by the Serbian irregular military.

EU actions and Bush's recognition of Croatia, Slovenia, and Bosnia completed the dissolution of the Yugoslavian Federation. But during the remainder of 1992, neither the EU, the U.S., nor the UN devised effective measures to stop the fighting.

Different US Strategies Could Have Limited the Damage

Wayne Bert

Puzzlingly, the United States' reluctance to get involved in a no-win situation led to just that in Bosnia, the following viewpoint asserts. After three years of neither committing its forces nor arming the beleaguered Bosnians, the United States ended up sending troops anyway. Early and preemptive air strikes could have halted Serb attacks and saved countless lives, all without significant risk, the author contends. Wayne Bert has written numerous articles on international politics. He has taught at Wilmington College in Ohio and has served as a policy analyst in the office of the US Secretary of Defense.

SOURCE. Wayne Bert, "The New Ethos on Intervention," *The Reluctant Superpower: United States' Policy in Bosnia, 1991–95.* Houndmills and London: Macmillan, 1997, pp. 240–246. Reproduced with permission of Palgrave Macmillan.

There were alternatives to the policies that were followed in Bosnia. The alternatives were inadequate and risky, but they promised a reasonable chance of success, and could hardly have been less successful than the ones the US followed. There is a strong consensus that no political leader could have justified the early dispatch of troops to Bosnia for a long period of time. The perception of American interests in Yugoslavia in a post-Cold-War setting simply did not justify the long-term placement of troops in the field. There were, however, less costly but still workable strategies of coercion. A well-crafted package of credible threats, which the US was willing to enforce if its demands were not met, might well have made a big difference in the war.

In the summer of 1992, when Belgrade's role was prominent and obvious, bombing of supply depots, artillery, key bridges across the Drina River, and other strategic assets in Bosnian-Serb areas, Serbia and even in Belgrade itself if necessary, would have had a big impact on the war. At that time, Serbian momentum was not yet established, expectations of Western (and especially US) reactions were unformed, and UN troops were not in place. Sudden and substantial bombing would have been a shock to the Serbs, and combined with a serious effort to supply the Bosnians with arms and train them, would have probably had a profound effect on the whole conflict. Certainly it would have slowed the Serb momentum and allowed the Muslims to buy some time. Such action would also have put the Croats on notice that they could not treat Western preferences with impunity, but most importantly it would have raised grave doubts about the possibility of a Serb victory in the war. This would have

> Sudden and substantial bombing would have been a shock to the Serbs, and . . . would have probably had a profound effect on the whole conflict.

led the Croats to think twice about assisting the Serbs against the Bosnians, since they would not want to end up on the losing side of a confrontation. This awareness could have been crucial, since the Croatian choice of sides has been a significant factor in determining the outcome of the war. Given the opportunistic, as opposed to committed, nature of [Croatian leader Franjo] Tudjman's involvement in the conflict, it is hard to exaggerate the importance of this factor.

Because of the need to convince the public of the advisability of intervention, intervention prior to the summer of 1992 was not politically feasible. But that summer was the most appropriate time for the kind of offensive described above. By the time the [US president Bill] Clinton administration came to power in early 1993, there were UN troops in place, the Serbs and the Bosnian Serbs had established momentum toward their objectives and would have been harder to influence, and the near completion of the Vance-Owen peace plan was strengthening opposition to military action for fear that it might jeopardize the negotiations. Moreover, it would have been less humiliating for an aggressive power such as Serbia to be stopped in the early stages of action rather than later. At the earlier time, it can always be claimed that there was no intention to take further aggressive action at all.

Thus, if the West was to intervene effectively after the war had begun, it was important to move to stop Serb advances early rather than to attempt to roll back their gains later. As the war went on, the Bosnian Serbs formed an increasingly more complete view of US will and intentions, and it took stronger threats to get their attention as they constantly validated their assumption that the US was not willing to intervene. Opportunities for the use of force existed during the Clinton administration, but had to take account of the danger to UN troops, and to overcome the momentum of business as usual. Decisive action might have included, for instance, [former British foreign secretary and member of Parliament] David Owen's recommended strategy of first withdrawing UNPROFOR [UN Protection Force], then lifting the embargo and bombing.

The use of force, if implemented later in the conflict, needed to be directed primarily at the Bosnian Serbs alone, as [Serbian leader Slobodan] Milosevic began increasing cooperation with the West in an effort to curb the Bosnian Serbs and get relief from the sanctions. Europeans and Americans disagreed over the extent of that cooperation, but any policy needed to be calibrated to maximize his contribution to curbing the radicals among the Bosnian Serbs. The Dayton Agreement did just that.

Reasons for Inaction Were Flawed

There were three basic arguments given for not intervening. The first one, used consistently by the [President George H.W.] Bush administration, was that if the US was not prepared to follow through with escalation if one tactic (air strikes, for instance) did not accomplish the objectives, then it should not begin the use of force. . . . It is hard to see how US credibility would have been damaged any more by at least trying something, even if not successful. The humiliation of the West as the war went on certainly came to equal any loss of credibility that would have resulted from leaving the field after failed bombing missions.

A second argument was that the use of air strikes, but particularly lifting of the arms embargo, would have spread the war. This argument . . . is seldom spelled out in much detail, possibly because it is difficult to defend. The proponents of the view that lifting the embargo would have equalled spreading the conflict assumed that bringing more arms into the region would also have expanded it to more parties, eventually involving Kosovo, Macedonia, Albania, or possibly other states bordering the former Yugoslavia. But relying on the assumptions

US soldiers on patrol in Sarajevo in 1996. (Tom Stoddart Archive/Getty Images.)

of the interventionist paradigm—on which so many US officials like [Lawrence] Eagleburger and [Cyrus] Vance learned their trade—would suggest that using force against the Serbs would contain the war rather than spread it, since it would deter them from expanding their operations. And when the Croats, after quietly preparing their operations, attacked the Serbs and in a matter of days had driven them from Croatia, the war may have technically been widened, but it was also quickly over. And once serious NATO bombing began in late summer 1995, there were no signs of an expanding war.

Inherent in the European view was the belief that if the intensity of the war was controlled by limiting the amount and sophistication of the arms coming into the area, a negotiated settlement could be worked out. There is very little evidence to substantiate that view. The ability of the Bosnian Serbs to import sophisticated weapons more easily would have contributed, but probably not

The Kosovo Conflict Outlasted Bosnia's

While armed clashes broke out in Croatia and then in Bosnia, leading to half a decade of violent struggles, a parallel dispute simmered just to the south, in Kosovo, a province of Serbia.

Centuries ago, the area had become the center of the Serbian empire and the location of important Serbian religious sites. However, by the end of the nineteenth century, ethnic Albanians had surpassed Serbs as the dominant population within Kosovo.

In July 1990, ethnic Albanian legislators declared independence for Kosovo. A Serbian crackdown ensued, with brutal reprisals continuing through the 1990s. Official and irregular Serbian forces detained and executed tens of thousands of Kosovo Albanian men, raped women, displaced more than a million ethnic Albanians, and destroyed houses and towns. International attempts at peace negotiations failed. Beginning March 24, 1999, NATO air strikes hit sites within Serbia, eventually forcing a Serb withdrawal from Kosovo.

The United Nations took over administration of the province, enforced by up to 50,000 NATO troops. UN-backed settlement talks between Serbs and Albanians in Kosovo did not succeed, and on February 17, 2008, the province's legislature reaffirmed Kosovo's independence. Over the next few years, many nations recognized Kosovo as a separate country. Serbia did not.

Kosovo's world status was undercut in December 2010, when a two-year international inquiry concluded that Kosovo's prime minister ran a criminal gang whose activities included selling body organs extracted from Serbian prisoners executed in 1999.

substantially, to their will to keep fighting and to their military capabilities and, if accompanied by a vigorous bombing campaign, any effects favorable to the Serbs from lifting the embargo would have been offset. What was accomplished instead was to handicap the Bosnian government in the conflict and deprive the Serbs of an incentive to negotiate or to moderate their demands. After three years of war and failed negotiations in Bosnia, the threats either to lift the arms embargo (from the Congress) or to withdraw the UNPROFOR troops (from the Europeans) finally led the Clinton administration to the military option it had rejected for so long.

A third and related reason given for not intervening was the reluctance to 'take sides'. This argument was partially based on the assumption that the conflict was basically a civil war where all sides were at fault and to support one side at the expense of the other would only diminish the prospects for a negotiated settlement. The narrower and more credible version of this argument stated that regardless of who [was] at fault for initiating the war, neutrality on the part of the West was necessary in order to serve as honest brokers to end the war. This argument was more prevalent in Europe than in the US, where the Serbs from the beginning tended to be blamed for the conflict. The flaw in this argument is the assumption that negotiations could succeed when the Serbs were winning and had reason to think they could make progress in obtaining their objectives. Third party mediation succeeds best when motivation and capabilities on both sides are similar, pushing both sides to settle. This certainly was not the case in the former Yugoslavia. The tendency for the US to talk tough but do nothing encouraged the Bosnian Serbs to believe they could make further gains, and paradoxically it encouraged the Bosnians to hope help was on the way.

> " The tendency for the US to talk tough but do nothing encouraged the Bosnian Serbs.

The United States Reacts Merely with Concern

Until recently, Bosnian policy, for both the Bush and the Clinton administrations, had been a dismal failure. In mid-1995, after four years of war in Yugoslavia, of which three years were in Bosnia, large numbers of dead and wounded and large percentages of the population existing as refugees, we were roughly back to square one, with the war still in full swing, the main actors in the conflict still fielding effective fighting forces, and the West still debating whether to conduct air strikes and lift the arms embargo. The crux of the problem was the inability of both the leadership and the public to face up to the need for hard choices. The Bush administration from the beginning did not even try to reconcile the yawning gap between its talk and its action. What was lacking was the courage to tell the American people that there were only two ways to end the war. One was to allow the military action between the parties on the ground to play itself out until one party could no longer sustain the losses and was forced to sue for surrender, or until both had had enough and reached a stalemate that forced a settlement. The second solution was Western intervention that tilted the balance of forces until a stable solution could be sold to or imposed on the warring parties.

Instead, the leadership tried to have it both ways. For most of the Clinton administration the rhetoric has been out of line with the military policy, but that policy has resulted in numerous twists and turns that confused all observers in the short run, but developed a remarkable consistency in the long run. Both the Bush and Clinton administration's policy was to placate the public by reacting to crises and showing concern, but refusing to do anything to change the situation in Bosnia, since that would involve costs and risks they were not willing to take. Thus, after years of war, in mid-1995 we were still dealing with some of the same decisions that dogged the leadership in the summer of 1992—only this time, it was clear that the policy of the status quo could not continue.

One of the most puzzling aspects of the Bosnian involvement was the willingness of the US leadership to play a passive role in the war, to countenance aggression and atrocities on the ground, literally in the presence of UN troops, to put up with (either directly or through the Western representative on the ground, UNPROFOR) incredible humiliation as the Serbs defied the West again and again, breached diplomatic protocol, and generally made fools of both Western military and diplomatic personnel. This can be partially but not entirely explained by the post-Cold-War changes in the international system and the resistance of public opinion to engage in a costly involvement. But this behaviour is doubly puzzling considering that a considerable number of the Western leadership were veterans of the Cold War who had been involved in going 'eyeball to eyeball' with the Russians and were willing to take the risk of doing so, seemingly with little reservation. These same leaders now could countenance three years of lies, deception and atrocities from the Serbs and still expect that any day, with no significant military pressure, a negotiated solution would be found. People who had believed in promoting a balance of power, avoiding power vacuums, arming rebel forces and promoting arms sales all over the world during the Cold War were suddenly in favor of arms embargoes to keep the level of violence low by preventing the victimized from defending themselves. All the while it was argued it was necessary not to take sides in the conflict and to keep channels of communications open. Some of these leaders endorsed the censure of Serbian leaders for war crimes, while still refusing to treat the Serbian military

> "The Serbs defied the West again and again . . . and generally made fools of both Western military and diplomatic personnel."

organization significantly differently from the Bosnians on the ground.

Such behavior toward the enemy during the Cold War, when the enemy was well defined and our purpose was clear, would have resulted in loud outcries from the opposition and the public, removal of the offending officials from office at the next election, and much wailing and lamentation in the press about the failure of the national leadership to defend the nation's interests. As it happened, only the last followed from this behavior during the Bosnian conflict. Some commentators, editorialists, and opposition were outraged, but most of the public and much of the opposition appeared to be at most only mildly upset about the state of US policy in Bosnia. Clearly the environment in which foreign policy was made had changed drastically. Still, the equanimity with which the West accepted humiliation and contempt from the Serbs was disturbing and puzzling.

In spite of the obsessive focus on the Vietnam experience throughout the Bosnian War, therefore, the West ended up in a stalemated situation somewhat analogous to Vietnam. In mid-1995, as the Serbs became bolder, taking hostages and invading 'safe areas' while the West stood by appearing increasingly helpless and incompetent, the UNPROFOR soldiers began to look more and more like hostages to the war. A realization grew that the troops might need to be withdrawn, and that to accomplish that action would require the temporary insertion of US troops. But this was what US policy had aimed at preventing for over three years. Refusing either to commit the force that might have turned the situation around, or to admit Western helplessness and provide the Bosnians with the tools to do the job themselves, the West tried to have it both ways and ended up accomplishing little toward ending the conflict or resolving the issues at stake.

Systematic Rape Was a Serbian War Tactic

M. Cherif Bassiouni and Marcia McCormick

During the conflict in Bosnia, all factions committed sexual violence to some extent. But only the Serbs used it systematically to drive entire populations from their homes, according to the authors of the following viewpoint. Frequent brutal rapes, degradation, and humiliation were at the least condoned by Serb commanders and appeared to have been planned from the start of the conflict. M. Cherif Bassiouni was a law professor and president of the International Human Rights Law Institute at DePaul University. He was chairman of the UN commission established to investigate human rights violations in the former Yugoslavia. Marcia McCormick, who was an assistant attorney general for the State of Illinois and who worked at the law institute at DePaul, is a law professor at St. Louis University School of Law. This viewpoint is drawn from a report by an investigative commission established by the United Nations.

SOURCE. M. Cherif Bassiouni and Marcia McCormick, "The Findings: The Use of Sexual Violence as an Instrument of War," *Sexual Violence: An Invisible Weapon of War in the Former Yugoslavia.* Chicago: International Human Rights Law Institute, DePaul University, 1996, pp. 15–23. Used by permission of the authors.

The database study and the field investigation [of a UN commission] support a single conclusion: sexual violence was not merely a by-product of the conflict in Bosnia but a tactic of the war. It was deliberately and systematically employed as a tool of "ethnic cleansing."

This conclusion is suggested by a number of recurrent patterns, common threads connecting the incidents of sexual violence, and several other significant factors that stood out in the course of the investigations and data analysis.

The strategic objective of forcibly removing civilian population from certain areas was necessary to achieve the political goal of "Greater Serbia." Various means of violence, terror, and intimidation were used. Its immediate purpose of terrorizing the targeted civilian population is obvious. It was also intended to insure that the victims and their families would not return to the cities, towns and villages where these crimes had occurred. Beyond that was the insidious long-term consequence of destroying families and communities.

> Serbs ran most of the detention camps where sexual violence took place.

This became obvious when the same patterns of behavior aimed at publicly humiliating the immediate victims of sexual violence and their families were repeated throughout distant territories and over more than one year. None of that could have occurred spontaneously. When coincidences are so frequently repeated, they cease to be that. Some reports indicated that such a plan had already been established in August 1991 and before the war started.

Another curious fact remains perplexing. Why is it that between May 1992 and June 1993, when most of these rapes reportedly occurred, the Serbs who were accused of them did so little to deny the allegations? According to some, it suited their purposes for such stories to be spread. But when world-wide media coverage, from December 1992 to May 1993, averaged some 500 stories a month, the number of such reported crimes was sharply reduced. Analysis and hypothesis about these and other observations of this tactic of war will surely continue to develop over the years to come.

Patterns of Sexual Violence Emerge

In its analysis of the database at DePaul's International Human Rights Law Institute, and in its own field interviews, the Commission gathered reports of sexual violence committed by all of the warring factions in the conflict, and suffered by diverse ethnic groups: Bosnian Muslims, Bosnian Serbs, Bosnian Catholics, Croatian Catholics, Croatian Serbs, Croatian Muslims and others. The great majority of victims were Bosnian Muslim, and the great majority of reported perpetrators were Bosnian Serb. Serbs ran most of the detention camps where sexual violence took place; these were also the sites of torture and murder, and many were surrounded by mass graves. The camps are located in a strategic arc joining Serbia with Bosnia and Herzegovina and Croatia, along the Drina and Sava rivers. These areas are not only closest to Serbia proper, they also have the highest concentration of ethnic Serbs—a fact of strategic importance to the ultra-nationalists seeking to establish a "Greater Serbia."

The information collected by the Commission revealed similarities in sexual violence committed across widely dispersed geographic areas. Five basic patterns of sexual violence emerged, tied to the military activity that was occurring in an area at the same time.

Sexual Violence with Looting and Intimidation. The first pattern was seen before widespread fighting broke out in a region. As tensions grew, members of the ethnic group controlling the local government began to terrorize their neighbors. Paramilitaries, other individuals, or gangs of men would break into a house, intimidate the residents, steal their property, beat them, and sexually assault the women, often in front of family members.

One reported case, for example, was that of an older Bosnian woman from a devout Muslim family. Militiamen compelled a drunk, 19-year-old Serb boy to rape her in the public square while her family and neighbors were forced to watch. The boy was apparently too drunk to succeed, and the event was made into a huge mockery by the militiamen, to the greater embarrassment of the village. One Bosnian Croat woman was gang-raped by eight soldiers in front of her six-year-old sister and her five-month-old daughter. . . .

A subset of this pattern was peculiar to one area of Bosnia and Herzegovina and Croatia, where a Croatian paramilitary group roamed the countryside, kidnapping primarily Bosnian Serb women from their homes. The women were taken away, raped repeatedly by groups of up to 15 men, and then abandoned.

Sexual Violence During Fighting. The second pattern of sexual violence occurred in conjunction with widespread fighting. When forces attacked a town or village, they gathered the population and separated them by sex and age. Some women were raped and sexually assaulted in their homes as the attacking forces secured the area. Others were selected after the roundup and raped and sexually assaulted publicly.

One witness, for example, saw an elderly woman and others raped in front of relatives and as many as 100 detained villagers. After such incidents the population of the village would be transported to detention camps.

Sexual Violence in Detention Facilities. A third pattern occurred in makeshift detention facilities or other sites, euphemistically called refugee "collection centers." After the population was rounded up in a town or village, men and women would be separated. Men of fighting age were tortured and executed or sent off to camps and fields to work for their captors. Women generally were sent to separate camps where soldiers, camp guards, paramilitaries, and even civilians were allowed to pick out women, take them away, and rape and sexually assault them. Guards would sometimes scour the crowded rooms by night, shining flashlights into faces, choosing victims randomly, and terrorizing the entire population of the camp. Afterwards, the women were either killed or returned to the camp, where they were eventually released in prisoner exchanges.

Though this was the predominant pattern in detention camps, there were also many reports that women were raped and sexually assaulted in front of other detainees, or that detainees were forced to rape and sexually assault one another. In some cases, the camp commander himself participated or watched. Gang-rapes were often reported in this setting, and many rapes were accompanied by beatings, torture, and many forms of humiliation. Detention camps also were the sites of torture, mass executions, and other humanitarian law violations.

> The sexual assault of men took place publicly, adding greatly to their humiliation.

In camps with mixed or male-only populations, men were also subjected to sexual assault. In one case, for example, a prisoner was forced to bite off the genitals of another. The sexual assault of men took place publicly, adding greatly to their humiliation.

Sexual Violence in Special Rape Camps. Survivors of some camps believe they were detained specifically so they could be sexually assaulted as a form of punishment. In these sites, all of the women were raped, and the abuse was routine; it was often accompanied by beatings

One of the buildings at the Omarska detention camp used to house and torture thousands of Muslims captured in the ethnic cleansing campaign of the Bosnian Serbs. (Shaul Schwarz/Getty Images.)

and torture, and frequently committed in front of other internees.

Sometimes additional factors heightened the victims' humiliation. In one camp, for example, girls were repeatedly raped and sexually assaulted in front of one another and were forced to drink alcohol, sit on mines, or jump out of windows. Similar incidents reportedly took place at camps run by Serbs, Croats, and Muslims. In many cases, the captors said they were trying to impregnate the women. One woman, for example, was told she would give birth to a Chetnik boy, a Serb ultra-nationalist, who would kill Muslims when he grew up. Hospitals in Sarajevo, Tuzla, and Zenica saw a sharp increase in abortions during 1992 and 1993. However, many women who became pregnant in the camps were detained until it was too late for them to abort. More than 120 forced impregnations were documented.

Sexual Violence in "Bordello" Camps. The last pattern was that of camps, often called bordellos, created expressly to hold women for sexual use by men returning from the front lines. Women would be collected from their homes and from camps and taken to hotels or private houses, where they were forced to provide sexual services for soldiers and civilians. Unlike other camps, the goal of detaining women in these facilities seemed to be not to harm or punish them, but to provide sex to men. Also unlike the other camps, the women at the bordello camps generally were killed rather than exchanged.

One such site was a small rooming house near Sarajevo, where Muslim and Catholic Croat women were kept for the "pleasure" of Serb fighters. One account describes this facility as a "convenience hotel" where, in a striking illustration of what [political theorist] Hannah Arendt termed "the banality of evil," a guard served as innkeeper, routinely dispensing keys to the rooms where the women were held. There the fighters would express their "superiority" and power by sexually assaulting the women. One paramilitary fighter who was tried and convicted by a Bosnian military court recalls going repeatedly to the "bordello," taking any woman he pleased, keeping her as long as he wished, and then killing her. Asked why he killed the women when he could easily have released them without anyone knowing, he replied, "I was told to do it."

One particularly tragic case was that of an 11-year-old girl from Foca, Bosnia, who became virtually catatonic after giving birth through forced impregnation. Two other slightly older girls from wealthy or professional families had also been taken to the same house and held for ransom where other young girls were also detained. There, for more than eight months, the girls were raped repeatedly by several guards, visiting friends, and the guards' commander. But a subsequent commander at this house put an end to the rapes by training a machine gun on the guards. A year after their ordeal, the older girls, determined to see justice done, courageously told their stories. Another case involved a woman who was raped under detention and then made to run naked in the town's main street. Another instance reported was that of high school girls being raped by their classmates brought in by military personnel to engage in this crime. These and many other stories were reported or told in person to investigators.

Rape Targets Were Chosen by Ethnicity

Some common threads run through the reported cases, regardless of the site or context in which they took place. For example:

Ethnic Motivation. Every reported case of sexual violence occurred in conjunction with efforts to displace civilians of a targeted ethnic group from the area. Reports of rape and sexual assault among members of the same ethnic group are few, and all have some cross-ethnic component. For example, some victims had sheltered members of the targeted ethnic group and others were married to a member of that group. Nearly all reports reveal some ethnic motivation. Still, there were many cases where women were protected by individuals of the same ethnic group as their attackers. Men sometimes took women out of the camps to protect them from sexual violence, told other guards or soldiers that the women were "taken," or helped them escape. Women often hid other women or brought them contraceptives.

> Sexual violence was often conducted in a manner that intensified the shame and humiliation of the assault.

Shame. Sexual violence was often conducted in a manner that intensified the shame and humiliation of the assault—for the victim, the family, and the entire community. Family members were forced to rape one another, victims were abused in front of their children, and victims were raped in public places or in front of other detainees. Large groups of men subjected women to multiple or gang-rapes and sexual assaults, and used objects such as rifles to assault them.

Men as well as women were subject to humiliation through sexual assault. They were forced to rape women, to perform oral sex on guards and on each other, and to perform other sex acts on one another. They also suffered castrations, circumcisions, and other sexual mutilations.

Brutality. Sexual assaults were often extremely brutal. Victims were assaulted with foreign objects like broken bottles, guns, and truncheons. Castrations were performed through crude means, including teeth and wires.

Broader Violations. Acts of sexual violence frequently took place in the context of other humanitarian law violations, including kidnappings, torture, and mass executions.

Targeting. Perpetrators targeted for rape not only young women and virgins, but community leaders and professional women. In one town, for example, Serbs held and repeatedly raped three extraordinarily courageous Bosnian Catholic women: a lawyer, a physician, and a judge. All have now spoken publicly and encouraged others to do so. The lawyer has recounted that every time she was raped, her tormentors would ask her if she was "broken"; each time she answered, "You will never break me."

Forced Impregnation. Those committing rape often told their victims that they had to become pregnant and held them in custody until it was too late for the victims to have an abortion. They told the women that they would have children of the perpetrator's ethnicity, a living reminder of what had happened to them.

Intention. Some perpetrators said they had been ordered to rape victims. Others said they were doing it so that the victims and their families would never want to return to the area. Some said that if the crime were ever disclosed, the perpetrators would hunt the women down and kill them. Camp commanders often knew about the sexual violence and sometimes participated in it.

Political and Military Leaders Were Involved

Some incidents of sexual violence were certainly opportunistic, carried out by individuals or small groups without direct orders or an overall policy. Many more cases, however, appear to be part of a larger picture whose recurrent patterns and common characteristics—over an extended period of time and more than 1,000 kilometers of borders separating Bosnia Government forces and Bosnian Serbs—strongly suggest a systematic policy to use sexual violence as an instrument of war.

The crimes could not have occurred in such consistent patterns, for so long, and in so many different places without some planning—and without the consent of the military and political leadership. While this remains to be definitively proven, it is strongly supported by the large number of incidents that occurred in detention camps—about 600 out of about 1,100 reported cases. These cases were not random; they required organization and coordination. They show that camp commanders had a policy of at least tolerating sexual violence and of deliberately failing to exercise control over the people under their authority. The highest levels of military and political leadership had to know what was occurring, and they are criminally responsible, at the very least, for failing to prevent the crimes and punish the perpetrators.

A curious finding adds credence to this interpretation and suggests, further, that high-level leaders deliberately planned the use of sexual violence. The reported incidents of sexual violence in the Commission's database took place between 1991 and 1993. The majority of these crimes occurred from April to November 1992, decreasing significantly in 1993. The number of media reports lagged just behind this curve, increasing from a handful of stories in the spring of 1992 to more than 1,000 worldwide in January and February 1993. Apparently, when media attention reached a critical mass, the number of incidents declined.

> [The] policy behind the use of sexual violence . . . , as practiced by the Serbs, was dramatically effective.

Was the media simply slow in catching up with violations in this terrible conflict? Or did pressure from worldwide media attention *cause* the violators to stop? Or—yet another possibility—did the violators feel that, with the worldwide publicity, they had achieved the purposes for which the sexual violence was being carried out? The last two explanations would indicate that commanders could control the perpetrators of sexual violence. And if that is the case, their failure to exercise control strongly supports the view that, there was, in fact, a policy behind the use of sexual violence.

This policy, as practiced by the Serbs, was dramatically effective. It used violence and terror, enhanced by humiliation and publicity, to force entire populations from their homes and prevent their return to the scene of their victimization. This was the key to ethnic cleansing. While the Commission heard allegations of rape and other crimes committed by Bosnian Muslims and Croatians against Serb women—crimes whose seriousness must not be ignored—there was no similar indication of a *policy* of sexual violence by the Bosnian and Croatian governments.

The use of sexual violence has been widespread in the conflict in the former Yugoslavia. While it has been used by all the warring factions, the majority of victims have been Bosnian Muslim, and the majority of perpetrators have been Bosnian Serb. It was this group that used rape as part of a policy of terror and violence designed to achieve ethnic cleansing.

The Commission identified several different patterns of sexual violence, involving victims both in and out of detention. The Commission also discovered many similarities in the conduct of perpetrators, in diverse areas throughout Bosnia and Herzegovina, between April 1992 and June 1993. The number of incidents decreased significantly in 1993, possibly in response to media attention and worldwide opprobrium.

While some of the sexual violence occurred sporadically, most of it was systematic and widespread, carried out in connection with efforts to displace the civilian population of a targeted ethnic group from a particular area. Sometimes field military and camp commanders explicitly ordered their subordinates to commit acts of sexual violence. In these cases, the individual commander's criminal responsibility is unequivocal. In other cases, field and camp commanders failed to prevent sexual violence and did not punish perpetrators when their crimes were disclosed. This is a violation of a commander's duties and makes the commander criminally responsible under international law. Indeed, the responsibility can be followed all the way up the chain of command, to those who planned the policy while pretending to know nothing about it—a practice known as "plausible deniability." These are the cases that must be carefully established—with facts, patterns, and policies—before the International Criminal Tribunal for the Former Yugoslavia.

A UN Declaration Failed to Save Thousands of Lives in Srebrenica

Ivan Lupis

An area in Bosnia designated as a haven by the United Nations and guarded by UN peacekeeping troops was turned into a killing ground by Serb forces, according to the following viewpoint, which was given as testimony to the US Congress. All the evidence indicates that the slaughter around the town of Srebrenica, Bosnia and Herzegovina, in 1995 was planned well in advance and then carried out with horrifying thoroughness over several days. A former researcher for the Helsinki division of Human Rights Watch, Ivan Lupis works for the United Nations Office for the Coordination of Humanitarian Affairs. He has also worked for the International Crisis Group and the UN war crimes tribunal dealing with the Bosnia conflict.

SOURCE. Ivan Lupis, "Statement of Ivan Lupis, Researcher, Human Rights Watch," Mass Graves and Other Atrocities in Bosnia, hearing before the US Congress Commission on Security and Cooperation in Europe, December 6, 1995, pp. 4–8. www.csce.gov.

The following testimony is based on an investigation carried out by myself and a consultant from July 31 to August 23, 1995.

It describes the events leading up to, during, and immediately after the fall of the U.N.-designated safe area of Srebrenica, including gross violations of humanitarian law, as has been typical of Serbian military conduct to date. The fall of the town of Srebrenica and its environs to Serb forces in early July 1995 made a mockery of the international community's professed commitment to safeguard regions it declared to be safe areas.

U.N. peacekeeping officials were unwilling to heed requests for support from their own forces stationed within the enclave, thus allowing Serb forces easily to overrun it and, without interference from U.N. soldiers, to carry out systematic mass executions of hundreds, possibly thousands, of civilian men and boys, and to terrorize, rape, beat, execute, rob, and otherwise abuse civilians being deported from the area.

> No peace agreement will be stable without justice for human rights abuses.

The recent Dayton peace plan and the guarded optimism that has accompanied this apparent progress should not obscure the fact that no peace agreement will be stable without justice for human rights abuses. The atrocities described in this testimony, like the many others that have preceded them in the former Yugoslavia, require of the international community, and specifically the United States, a commitment to repatriation for victims and accountability for the perpetrators.

Before the war, approximately 37,000 people, 72 percent Muslim and 25 percent Serbs, lived in the Srebrenica municipality. When Bosnian Serb forces began their brutal campaign of ethnic cleansing with the help of the Yugoslav People's Army in eastern Bosnia in 1992, most areas quickly fell under Serb control. Most of the non-

Serb men either fled, were put into detention centers, or were indiscriminately killed.

Thousands of mostly Muslim refugees from other areas of eastern Bosnia flocked to places like Zepa, Gorazde, and Srebrenica, where territorial defense units succeeded in fending off Serb attacks. As a result of this sudden demographic shift, Srebrenica's population swelled to an estimated 55,000 to 60,000 people and remained under siege for more than 3 years.

On April 16, 1993, the U.N. Security Council adopted Resolution 819, declaring Srebrenica a safe area; and a cease-fire was signed on April 17. But in July 1995, there were numerous indications that Bosnian Serb forces were planning a summer offensive against Srebrenica. Access to U.N. convoys was increasingly restricted by Bosnian Serb forces, so that by late February and early March 1995, only one convoy per month was being allowed into the area to feed the approximately 39,000 people left in the enclave.

A U.N. official in Tuzla told us that this was a deliberate tactic used by the Serbs to weaken the population of the enclave in order to prepare the area for a final offensive. The incremental denial of food, water, electricity, and proper medical supplies by the Serbs over a long period of time should actually have been viewed as the true preparatory stages of the July assault on the enclave and should have served as a warning signal to the international community that the so-called U.N. safe area of Srebrenica was in danger.

UN Troops Were Overwhelmed

Prior to the offensive, Bosnian Serb forces also hampered peacekeeping effectiveness as well as troop rotations into the enclave. Two rotations of Dutch troops stationed in the enclave had been allowed to leave, but the Bosnian Serbs refused their replacements' entry. Thus, the entire pocket, civilians and UNPROFOR [UN Protection

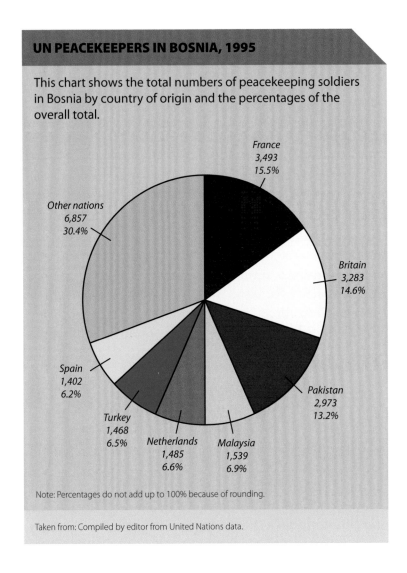

UN PEACEKEEPERS IN BOSNIA, 1995

This chart shows the total numbers of peacekeeping soldiers in Bosnia by country of origin and the percentages of the overall total.

France
3,493
15.5%

Other nations
6,857
30.4%

Britain
3,283
14.6%

Spain
1,402
6.2%

Pakistan
2,973
13.2%

Turkey
1,468
6.5%

Netherlands
1,485
6.6%

Malaysia
1,539
6.9%

Note: Percentages do not add up to 100% because of rounding.

Taken from: Compiled by editor from United Nations data.

Force] troops alike, were psychologically and physically exhausted weeks prior to the offensive.

Just two days before the attack, Bosnian Serb forces allowed one convoy carrying 100,000 liters of diesel fuel, an unprecedented amount, into the pocket. This fuel was then recaptured when the safe area fell. Given the embargo of the Bosnian Serbs, as well as their refusal to allow fuel into the enclave on previous occasions, this sudden influx of fuel should have been suspicious to the Dutch U.N. soldiers. Without the fuel, Bosnian Serb forces would not have been able later to bus tens of thousands of Muslims to Bosnian Government-controlled territory.

By July 5, approximately 5,000 Serb troops had surrounded the enclave with 50 artillery pieces and 15 to 20 battle vehicles and launched a full-scale offensive on Srebrenica at 3:15 A.M. on July 6. The shelling was too heavy to count the number of detonations, but U.N. estimates were in the thousands. Serb troops began taking control of U.N. observation posts one by one, and by the time the offensive was over, 55 U.N. troops had been taken hostage.

> The shelling was too heavy to count the number of detonations.

Dutch soldiers within the enclave requested close air support from the U.N. commanders, but the date of the request remains disputed. U.N. officials interviewed by us deny that Dutch troops in the safe area requested close air support before July 10. Other evidence, however, suggests that Dutch troops in the enclave acted sooner and believe that close air support might have dissuaded Serb forces from pressing their offensive.

According to the Dutch, close air support was requested on July 6. That request and subsequent ones were repeatedly turned down by the commander of U.N. peace forces in former Yugoslavia, Bernard Janvier. On July 10, according to UNHCR [UN High Commissioner for Refugees] estimates, approximately 30,000 people began to evacuate Srebrenica and move back to the northern part of the enclave toward the U.N. base in Potocari, a village located halfway between Srebrenica and Bratunac.

Finally, on July 11, two days after Serbian forces had driven through Srebrenica, four fighter planes took part in an attack which resulted in the destruction of one Serb tank. Bosnian Serb commander Ratko Mladic threatened to fire on the Dutch compound and the civilian population of Srebrenica and to execute Dutch peacekeeping hostages if more air strikes were carried out.

The air strikes were not repeated and the U.N. effort to save the U.N. safe area of Srebrenica shifted to damage control. Now, due to my limited amount of time, I have to skip over what happened with the women, children, and elderly people in Potocari and move on to the massacres because this is the focus of this testimony. . . .

Refugees Walk into Ambushes

As Srebrenica was falling, the overwhelming majority of military-aged men and boys and a smattering of women and children gathered in separate locations in order to make the journey through Bosnian Serb-held areas to reach Bosnian Government-controlled territory. The majority of the persons in this group of 12,000 to 15,000 trekkers were civilians. Men and boys interviewed by us stated that only between 3,000 to 4,000 of them were armed. After the U.N. failed to defend the safe area of Srebrenica, the enclave's military-aged men no longer trusted the UNPROFOR troops, nor did they believe their safety would be guaranteed by them. They formed a column which stretched for approximately ten kilometers and walked in a vulnerable formation because they had been warned of a mined terrain.

During the trek, the column was exposed to numerous attacks and ambushes by Serbian forces, during which violations of humanitarian law were committed. A displaced person I interviewed vividly described the horrific ordeal which the men and boys experienced. He mentioned:

> After about three kilometers, we encountered our first ambush at a stream. The center of our column was hit by anti-aircraft machine guns and mortars. Around 200

people died just from that. The Cetniks [which is a term used by many to describe nationalist Serbs] then came down from the hills, and about 2,000 men from the middle of the column got caught in the line of fire. The people at the front and back of the column scattered everywhere. I was in the middle and saw how the Serbs were shooting everyone and slaughtering us with bayonets.

> 'I was in the middle and saw how the Serbs were shooting everyone and slaughtering us with bayonets.'

Furthermore, during the nighttime and during the ambushes, Serb soldiers in civilian clothing managed to infiltrate the column, spreading disinformation and confusion, giving wrong directions, injecting men with what was believed to have been hallucinatory drugs, drawing groups and individuals away from the column, and opening fire on and executing people from within the column.

As the ambushes and infiltrating Serbs continued to pick away at the column, men and boys tried desperately to regroup after the ambush. The column eventually became smaller and smaller in number, and smaller groups were left behind and separated from the rest. Many men and boys surrendered, and several witnesses told us that they saw unarmed men shot in the process of surrendering.

We conducted interviews with a witness to a massacre in the Nova Kasaba/Konjevic Polje area and with four other persons who were sent to mass executions at two sites in the Karakaj area, a town north of Zvornik on the Bosnian-Serbian border. Mass summary executions were also carried out at at least two locations in the Bratunac area, and evidence points to the existence of two sites in the Kravice area as well.

The systematic nature of the operation, already described in the offensive, and the attack designed to break up the escaping column of men can be further adumbrated during the round-up phase of the dispersed trekkers. Serb forces strategically positioned themselves along major roads and rivers over which the men would have to cross in order to reach Bosnian Government territory. Serb forces apparently tried to capture as many men as possible before they could cross so that they could be detained at sites around Nova Kasaba and Konjevic Polje.

Survivors Describe Days of Massacres

As described in our reports, Serb forces communicated orders and instructions to the men by megaphones on how and where to surrender before they could reach the two roads. According to a displaced person, large massacres were carried out in this area. He recounted:

> The place was full of Cetniks so we hid in some high grass and waited. Muslims were coming down on the main road from everywhere giving themselves up. The Cetniks picked out Muslims who they either knew about or knew, interrogated them, and then made them dig pits which would be used as mass graves.
>
> During our first day there, the Cetniks killed approximately 500 people. They would just line them up and shoot them into the pits. The approximately 100 men whom they interrogated and who had dug the mass graves then had to fill them in. At the end of the day, they were ordered to dig a pit for themselves and line up in front of it. Then with M53 machine guns, they were shot into the mass graves.
>
> At dawn, it was still the same. A bulldozer arrived and dug up a pit which seemed to be about 30 meters long and about 15 meters wide, and they buried about 400 men alive. The men were encircled by Cetniks. Whoever tried to escape was shot. After that, they packed down the earth so it almost looked as good as new.

Photo on following page: A forensic expert works at one of the sites of mass burials from the Srebrenica killings. **(AP Photo/Amel Emeric.)**

In this area, many men and boys described the appearance of Bosnian Serb general Ratko Mladic, who oversaw parts of the operation being carried out. Moreover, they reported seeing Serb soldiers dressed in U.N. garb driving around in white U.N. armored personnel carriers.

The fact that four of the survivors were detained in and transited through the Nova Kasaba/Konjevic Polje area and were then bused to Karakaj via Bratunac further suggests that the campaign carried out by the Serb forces was systematic in nature.

A number of citizens of Bratunac and its surrounding villages told about the violent deaths of a large number of men from Srebrenica. The villagers' accounts were consistent in many details, including the place and the method of execution. One woman, a resident of Serbia proper, reportedly said that she had just been to visit her brother-in-law, who was a Bosnian Serb soldier.

> 'He and his friends are quite open about what is going on. . . . They are killing Muslim soldiers.'

"He and his friends are quite open about what is going on," the woman exclaimed. "They are killing Muslim soldiers. They said they killed 1,600 yesterday alone and estimated in all they had killed about 4,000. They said they were in a big hurry so they were shooting most of them."

In the Karakaj area, men were ordered to get out of the trucks in groups of five or ten and line up in front of the Serb soldiers who fired on them. Four survivors disclosed details which indicate that the mass executions were well-planned and systematically carried out. For example, all noted that for extended periods of time, trucks pulled up to the sites and dropped off loads of prisoners. Firing squads would execute several groups and were then ordered to walk among the corpses to make sure everyone was dead. The presence of bulldozers, which pushed the dead bodies onto tractor-trailers, indicated that the Serb authorities had prepared for a large number of persons to be executed at the sites. . . .

Thousands of Civilian Men and Boys Killed

The July 1995 attack on the U.N.-declared safe area of Srebrenica by Serb forces was planned well in advance, and abuses perpetrated after the fall of the enclave were systematic and well-organized. According to the UNHCR, up to 8,000 men, including boys as young as twelve years old, remain missing; and many are believed to have been killed or executed.

Although the U.N. member states and U.N. officials have been ready to condemn war crimes and crimes against humanity in the former Yugoslavia, little has been done to prevent or stop such abuses from taking place. Between August and October 1995, while the United States carried out active negotiations with Serbian leader Slobodan Milosevic, systematic ethnic cleansing continued to be carried out against tens of thousands of non-Serbs in northwestern Bosnia.

Two thousand men, civilians who had never engaged in armed resistance, disappeared as their families were expelled into Bosnian Government-controlled territory. Numerous witnesses reported seeing Serbian-based special forces of Arkan operating in the area. Arkan is the nom-de-guerre [pseudonym] of Zeljko Raznatovic, a suspected war criminal from Serbia.

Moreover, we also obtained several testimonies and photographic evidence pointing to a mass execution of approximately 150 civilians, which took place in the end of September 1995.

The NATO Bombing Campaign Helped Bring Peace to the Balkans

Ryan C. Hendrickson

After the United Nations' efforts failed to stop the conflict in and around Bosnia, the US-led NATO (North Atlantic Treaty Organization) coalition finally used its air power, according to the author of the following viewpoint. The bombing of Serbs in Bosnia, done with UN concurrence, was the action that led to a peace agreement. The NATO campaign also led to new roles for the Western military alliance, the author asserts, including on-the-ground peacekeeping outside its traditional geographic area. Ryan C. Hendrickson is a political science professor at Eastern Illinois University whose books include *Diplomacy and War at NATO*.

Early in the morning of 30 August 1995 NATO aircraft launched a series of precision strikes against selected targets in Serb-held Bosnia and

SOURCE. Ryan C. Hendrickson, "Crossing the Rubicon," *NATO Review*, Autumn 2005. www.nato.int.

Herzegovina. This heralded the start of Operation Deliberate Force, NATO's first air campaign, that lasted for two-and-a-half weeks, shattered Bosnian Serb communications and effectively ended the "out-of-area" debate that had dominated intra-Alliance discussions on NATO's role since the end of the Cold War.

Although extremely controversial at the time, a decade on it is clear that Operation Deliberate Force and the judicious use of air power was critical to bringing the Bosnian War to an end with enormous political consequences and obvious benefits for Bosnia and Herzegovina. In addition, though subsequently overshadowed by Operation Allied Force, the Alliance's much longer air campaign in Kosovo in 1999, Operation Deliberate Force may have contributed more to NATO's post-Cold War transformation than any other single event.

In spite of Bosnia and Herzegovina's eventual importance to NATO, the Alliance was slow to join international efforts to end fighting in the former Yugoslavia. When violence erupted in 1991, first the European Community and then the United Nations took the lead in seeking to halt the conflict and restore peace and stability. At the time, the United States had just led a UN-approved coalition to drive Saddam Hussein's Iraq out of Kuwait and there was great optimism about the United Nations' potential to promote a "new world order."

The Bosnian War proved an extremely sobering experience for the United Nations and all international institutions that became involved in negotiations to end the conflict. The UN Protection Force (UNPROFOR), which eventually grew to 38,000 troops, was tasked with delivering humanitarian assistance to those in need and providing "safe areas" in which civilians should not be harmed. But it was expected to remain politically neutral and was not mandated to enforce a particular settlement, since no settlement had been agreed. The phrase that encapsulated UNPROFOR's predicament at the time was

> The United Nations' blue berets were 'peacekeepers with no peace to keep.'

that the United Nations' blue berets were "peacekeepers with no peace to keep."

While UNPROFOR struggled to achieve its objectives, NATO was itself seeking to come to terms with the end of the Cold War. In 1991, at their Rome Summit, NATO heads of state and government agreed to a New Strategic Concept, enabling the Alliance to go beyond collective defence and to conduct new security missions, including peacekeeping, conflict-prevention and crisis-management activities. In this way, in 1994 and the first half of 1995, NATO used force in limited strikes against Bosnian Serb military targets in response to violations of various UN Security Council Resolutions. Under the military guidance of Supreme Allied Commander, Europe, General George Joulwan, the Alliance also helped police a UN arms embargo against the whole of the former Yugoslavia and economic sanctions against Serbia and Montenegro.

Frustrated, the UN Turned to NATO

NATO's early forays into Bosnia and Herzegovina failed to change the political realities on the ground and prompted many analysts to question the Alliance's relevance in the post-Cold War security environment. Many perceived NATO's role in the Balkans as especially troubling, given the extent of the humanitarian suffering taking place in what was after all NATO's backyard. In an oft-repeated refrain, both NATO supporters and NATO critics argued that the Alliance would have to go "out of area" or it would go "out of business."

As international media maintained blanket coverage of the conflict, dissatisfaction grew with the international community's piecemeal and inadequate response. Although most UNPROFOR soldiers served with distinction and 167 lost their lives in the course of the mission,

UNPROFOR's inability to influence the dynamics of the conflict enabled the Bosnian Serbs to make a mockery of the UN mission. Indeed, both NATO Secretary General Willy Claes and his predecessor Manfred Wörner became increasingly outspoken about the United Nations' inability to end the crisis and the need for NATO to take on a greater role. Despite this, the Allies themselves were unable to build the necessary political consensus for a more robust approach during 1994 and the first half of 1995 and continued to debate the most appropriate course of action.

NATO's inertia was, in part, a reflection of UNPROFOR's composition. Many Allies, including Canada, France and the United Kingdom, had deployed their own peacekeepers in UNPROFOR and feared that a more robust approach towards the Bosnian Serbs would produce a backlash against their troops. Meanwhile, the United States, which did not have troops on the ground, was pushing a "lift and strike" policy—lifting the arms embargo against the entire region that penalised in particular the Bosnian Muslims and striking the Bosnian Serb targets from the air.

> The turning point was the Srebrenica massacre of mid-July 1995: the single greatest atrocity of the Wars of Yugoslavia's Dissolution.

To be sure, US diplomatic pressure for change remained cautious. The deaths of eighteen US Army Rangers in an ambush in October 1993 in Mogadishu, Somalia, which effectively ended the UN peacekeeping mission to Somalia, continued to cast a long shadow over policy-making. Senior US officials and Pentagon planners had no intention of becoming engaged in another poorly planned operation risking combat casualties where clear national security interests were not at stake. Moreover, CIA analysts estimated that it would take thousands of ground troops to restore the peace.

Refugees from Kosovo arrive at a makeshift camp in Macedonia before moving on to a NATO camp. (Roger Lemoyne/Liaison/Getty Images.)

The turning point was the Srebrenica massacre of mid-July 1995: the single greatest atrocity of the Wars of Yugoslavia's Dissolution that resulted in the deaths of close to 8,000 Bosnian Muslim men and boys, shocked world opinion and galvanised Washington to steer NATO in a new direction. In US President Bill Clinton's White House, National Security Advisor Anthony Lake, who according to Ivo Daalder's *Getting to Dayton: The Making of America's Bosnia Policy* had long advocated a more robust approach, took the lead in pushing the Allies in a new direction.

The United States was not alone in urging a new, more robust Allied approach to the Bosnian War. Attitudes towards the Bosnian Serbs had been hardening even before the Srebrenica massacre, especially after UN peacekeepers, many of whom were French, were taken hostage in May 1995. In this way, French President Jacques Chirac was equally vocal about the need for a radically new and more interventionist policy.

Unanimity Came at Last

One critical policy change introduced in early August 1995 was a reworking of the "dual-key" arrangement, which had been established in 1993 to govern the use of force by NATO. The arrangement required that NATO military action be approved by both UN and NATO officials. Until August 1995, Yasushi Akashi, the UN Secretary-General's Special Representative in Yugoslavia, held the United Nations' key. After Srebenica, Akashi's key was given to UNPROFOR's military commander, French General Bernard Janvier. The NATO key was held by Admiral Leighton W. Smith, Commander of Allied Forces Southern Europe in Naples.

The event that triggered Operation Deliberate Force took place on 28 August 1995, when a Serb mortar fell upon a market place in Sarajevo, killing thirty-eight civilians and injuring eighty-five others. With General Janvier away at that time, British Lieutenant-General Rupert Smith turned the UN key in coordination with Admiral Smith, indicating that the Bosnian Serbs had yet again violated a UN Security Council Resolution and that this time NATO would respond with force.

Operation Deliberate Force was launched as soon as the last UNPROFOR troops left Bosnian Serb territory. The bombing was briefly interrupted due to a cease-fire negotiated by General Janvier on 1 September, but it resumed in the early hours of 5 September. Almost all the then 16 NATO Allies contributed in some way to the campaign, which involved a total of 3,515 sorties and the dropping of 1,026 bombs at 338 individual targets. There

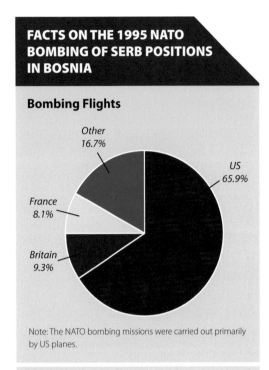

FACTS ON THE 1995 NATO BOMBING OF SERB POSITIONS IN BOSNIA

Bombing Flights

Other 16.7%

US 65.9%

France 8.1%

Britain 9.3%

Note: The NATO bombing missions were carried out primarily by US planes.

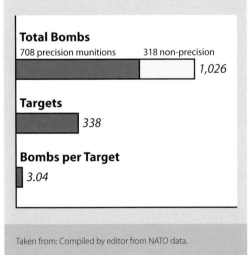

Total Bombs

708 precision munitions   318 non-precision

1,026

Targets

338

Bombs per Target

3.04

Taken from: Compiled by editor from NATO data.

were no NATO casualties, though a French Mirage 200K was shot down on the first day of the campaign and the crew captured by the Bosnian Serbs.

Among the many individuals involved in Operation Deliberate Force, NATO Secretary General Willy Claes played an especially influential role behind the scenes. Although Claes' personal political problems in Belgium have cast a shadow over his legacy and obliged him to leave NATO after less than a year and a half in office, he can take much credit for ensuring that the Alliance saw Deliberate Force through to a successful conclusion.

In his short period as NATO Secretary General, Claes showed himself to be a determined leader who was prepared to keep the North Atlantic Council in session for hours until consensus could be reached, especially in the lead-up to Deliberate Force. According to Richard Holbrooke's account in *To End a War*, Claes also actively supported both of the Smiths when the keys were turned, allowing the air campaign to proceed without additional debate from the Allies. When General Janvier negotiated a temporary cease-fire with Bosnian Serb military commanders, Claes placed considerable diplomatic pressure on him, other UN officials and the North Atlantic Council to resume the air strikes, arguing that NATO had to demonstrate greater resolve to change attitudes on the ground.

Claes' relationship with General Joulwan was also important to the success of the air campaign. When General Joulwan requested political support to use Tomahawk missiles against Bosnian Serb military positions in Banja Luka, Claes backed him. The use of the Tomahawks in the early morning hours of 10 September generated some criticism, even among NATO Ambassadors, but today is considered by military analysts such as Colonel Robert C. Owen in *Deliberate Force: A Case Study in Effective Air Campaigning* to have been significant in demonstrating NATO's resolve and therefore likely to have helped bring the conflict to an end.

> In the wake of Operation Deliberate Force, the Bosnian Serbs . . . were more willing to negotiate.

In the wake of Operation Deliberate Force, the Bosnian Serbs found it increasingly difficult to retain territory they had held since the early months of the Bosnian War in the face of a concerted offensive involving Croatian as well as Bosnian Croat and Bosnian Muslim forces. As a result, they were more willing to negotiate an end to the war in talks that got under way in Dayton, Ohio, on 1 November than they had been earlier in the conflict. In effect, Operation Deliberate Force helped pave the way for the Dayton Peace Agreement, which succeeded in establishing the governing framework for Bosnia and Herzegovina that remains in place to this day.

Almost a decade since it came into force, the Dayton Peace Agreement has not managed to resolve Bosnia and Herzegovina's conflict and the peace process is yet to become self-sustaining. More than 7,000 troops, most of them deployed since December 2004 under the European Union's auspices, remain in the country and international administrators continue to play an intrusive role in Bosnian political life, frequently overruling local officials. Nevertheless, the Dayton Peace Agreement succeeded in ending Europe's bloodiest conflict since the

Second World War, which had taken more than 100,000 lives during the previous four years. And it gave Bosnians the opportunity to rebuild their country and with it a better future for themselves.

NATO's Role and Status Changed

Operation Deliberate Force also helped restore the credibility of both NATO and the wider international community. By intervening militarily in Bosnia and Herzegovina the Alliance had moved definitively out of area, that is beyond Allied territory. Moreover, NATO demonstrated that it was capable both of overseeing a successful multinational military campaign and of using force to achieve non-Article 5 objectives, that is objectives other than collective defence.

Under the terms of the Dayton Peace Agreement, NATO became involved in peacekeeping for the first time. The Alliance led a 60,000-strong Implementation Force or IFOR to oversee implementation of the accord's military aspects and ensure that the country did not slide back into war. Moreover, the Bosnian deployment generated a series of additional benefits, including, for example, the integration of some 2,000 Russian troops and officers into NATO-led structures. In a move that had seemed impossible only five years earlier, these soldiers worked side by side with their NATO peers for the next seven years.

Operation Deliberate Force also heralded a much wider NATO engagement in and commitment to the Balkans. In 1999, NATO again successfully used force against Slobodan Milosevic and his military forces with a 78-day air campaign to halt ethnic cleansing in Kosovo. That campaign was followed by the creation and deployment of another NATO-led peacekeeping mission, the Kosovo Force or KFOR, which remains deployed today. And in 2001, NATO intervened in the former Yugoslav Republic of Macedonia in a preventive capacity to head

Air Power Targeted Kosovo and Serbia

Four years after the NATO bombing campaign in Bosnia, the alliance used the same technique, for much the same reasons, in Kosovo and Serbia. The 1999 US-led attacks, however, were larger-scale and more controversial.

The later campaign, which lasted from March 24 to June 11, 1999, came after Serb forces failed to respond to diplomatic efforts to end violence in Kosovo. The Serb position was that Kosovo was part of Serbia and armed efforts were needed to end rebellion there.

NATO unleashed twenty-three thousand bombs and missiles against military installations as well as power plants, bridges, factories, and hospi-

tals, including in Serbia's capital city, Belgrade. In sum, the bombing led to a Serb withdrawal without any NATO combat fatalities and essentially brought an end to the Balkan warfare of the 1990s, but it also killed about five hundred civilians and caused massive disruption of civilian life.

Among the sites bombed was the Chinese embassy in Belgrade. The US apologized for the attack, which killed five people, calling it a mistake. However, NATO sources said the targeting was intentional because the Serb leader was thought to be in the embassy and the embassy was transmitting communications to Serb forces.

off another war and restore peace and stability to the region.

Although it took the Allies far too long to develop the necessary political consensus to intervene effectively in Bosnia and Herzegovina, once the Alliance decided to confront the causes of the conflict, it succeeded in rapidly ending the violence and then in developing the means to build peace. In this way, Operation Deliberate Force ushered in a new era for NATO, helping set the foundation for the much larger range of non-Article 5 missions that the Alliance is involved in today, and moving NATO way beyond the sole maintenance of its own collective defence.

The NATO Bombing Hurt the Cause of the Bosnian People

The Militant

> The bombing of Bosnia by the Western alliance is simply another imperialist action to gain influence in the Balkans, the authors of the following viewpoint assert. It is part of a historical pattern in which the governments of large countries claim to be humanitarian while actually trampling on peoples' rights and seeking economic domination. The better response to the Serb regime, the authors say, would be to help the working people of Bosnia wage their own battles. *The Militant* is a socialist newsweekly based in New York City.

SOURCE. *The Militant*, "Stop NATO Bombing in Bosnia," v. 59, no. 34, September 18, 1995. www.themilitant.com. Used by permission of The Militant.

Much newspaper print and television time is being used to push the view that the NATO bombing campaign under way advances the cause of the Bosnian people. *The Militant* has taken a stance—and urges its readers to do so as well—that the imperialist military intervention in the former Yugoslavia holds no benefits for working people in the region or anywhere else.

Far from ending the conflict, the use of military force and threats of wider war set back the fight by the Bosnian people for self-determination and national sovereignty.

The White House and U.S. Congress justify the bombing by citing humanitarian concerns for the besieged people of Sarajevo and other Bosnian cities.

Many working people and youth are swayed by such claims because of their natural human sympathy for the plight of the people of Bosnia. But the government of the United States, as well as those of Britain, France, Italy, Germany, and Japan, have a long history of professing humanitarianism to carry out brutal assaults, and using their massive armed forces to advance their imperialist interests and trample on the rights of working people the world over.

> [The Bosnian people] are not helpless victims who must rely on Washington for salvation.

The U.S. invasions of Haiti (1994), Panama (1989–90), and Grenada (1983); London's war against Argentina to maintain its colonization of the Malvinas islands (1982); and the U.S.-led war against the people of Iraq in 1990–91 are some of the most recent examples. They were carried out under the pretext of defending human rights and democracy.

Imperialist intervention is often disguised with the fig leaf of the United Nations. That was the case in Somalia (1992–94); during the overthrow of the government of Patrice Lumumba in the Congo (now Zaire) by UN forces in 1961; and in the 1950–53 Korean War, when Washington used the blue flag of the United Nations to carry out its massive invasion and partition the peninsula against the will of the vast majority of the Korean people.

The rival imperialist powers of North America and Europe are seeking ways to intervene in the Yugoslav war, place their stamp on the outcome of events, and thus increase their influence in the Balkans. They are driven to do this by increased conflicts among themselves in the context of a world capitalist economy marked by declining profit rates and stiffening competition for markets. They seek to reinforce the fracturing of the former Yugoslavia and eventually overturn the nationalized property relations and reestablish capitalism.

The US Peace Plan Is a Power Grab

In Bosnia, the U.S. government is using its military might to set in stone what has been already carved out by the massive spilling of blood of the Bosnian people—the partition of that former Yugoslav republic. Washington is doing so to increase the edge it has already gained over its imperialist rivals in the Balkans. It has outdistanced Bonn [Germany] in its support for the regime in Croatia. And NATO, the U.S. military arm in Europe, is currently calling the shots over decisions for military intervention in Bosnia.

Now the [US president Bill] Clinton administration is peddling the idea of using up to 25,000 U.S. ground troops as part of a 50,000-strong occupation force to enforce its "peace plan." This is simply naked imperialist military intervention in the former republics of the Yugoslav workers state. The "humanitarianism" of Washington and other imperialist powers is exposed as crocodile tears by their backing of Zagreb's "ethnic cleansing," and the shutting of their borders and mistreatment of hundreds of thousands of refugees from the war.

The chief culprit for the murderous conflict in the former Yugoslavia is the regime of Slobodan Milosevic in Serbia. This gangsterous regime of would-be capitalists and its allies in Bosnia pioneered the "ethnic cleansing" in their drive to grab land and resources. The regime of Franjo Tudjman in Croatia followed suit.

The petty-bourgeois and aspiring bourgeois layers in Belgrade, Zagreb, and elsewhere are interested only in safeguarding their own privileges, diverting workers from acting in their own class interests, and continuing the fruitless attempt to be welcomed as equal partners into the world capitalist system.

But because of the historic conquests of the Yugoslav revolution in the 1940s, many working people in all the republics—Serb, Croat, Bosnian, and others—oppose

The Serbian-occupied village of Planeje, Kosovo, was destroyed by NATO air strikes. **(Tyler Hicks/ Getty Images.)**

being forcibly divided along national lines. From the beginning of the bloody war in 1991, many workers, farmers, and youth in Yugoslavia have shown by their own actions the potential they possess to resist the slaughter.

Tens of thousands of people in Bosnia have taken up arms to defend their right to self-determination, halt the horrors of "ethnic cleansing," and put an end to the onslaught. They are not helpless victims who must rely on Washington for salvation. Working people the world over should support this fight, including the right of the Bosnian army to obtain weapons wherever it can. But the NATO bombings, and the support for Washington's military assault by the government of Alija Izetbegovic in Sarajevo, set back this fight.

Instead, the labor movement should demand:

- Stop the NATO bombing and end all plans for further military intervention!
- Support Bosnia's self-determination!
- Lift the arms embargo and economic sanctions against all the former Yugoslav republics!
- Open the U.S. and other imperialist borders to the refugees from the Yugoslav carnage!

International Criminal Tribunals Are Tools for Peace

Richard J. Goldstone

The international court that tried participants in the Bosnian conflict was neither unique nor unprecedented. As shown earlier in South Africa, Rwanda, and elsewhere, such a tribunal not only convicts war criminals, it demolishes false denials and discourages future violence, the author of the following viewpoint contends. Through such tribunals victims receive justice, and bringing the truth to light vindicates the survivors. A former judge in South Africa, where he fought against its policy of apartheid, Richard J. Goldstone was the chief prosecutor for the international tribunals dealing with war crimes in Rwanda and the former Yugoslavia.

I t is now generally recognized that democracy depends not only on regular fair elections but [also] on respect for the rule of law. We should not forget

---

SOURCE. Richard J. Goldstone, "Ceremonial Address," Central European University website, November 3, 2009. www.ceu.hu.

that [Adolf] Hitler, [Slobodan] Milosevic and [Robert] Mugabe came to power in consequence of elections that were held to be free and fair. It was the subversion of the rule of law that led to their oppressive regimes. I need not use time today to discuss the rule of law in its domestic setting. We can all agree, I am certain, that at the core of the doctrine lies the separation of powers between the legislature, the executive and the judiciary, the independence of the judiciary and an independent legal profession, equality before the law and due process. If any of those principles is compromised, the consequences for democracy are devastating and destructive.

How do those principles apply at the international level? The first and most obvious difference is that there is no international legislature and no international executive. There is, however, a fast-growing international judiciary. Is this a paradox? Not really. Although there is no international legislature, there are certainly international laws. Their sources are primarily international treaties and customary international law. They are based upon the voluntary agreement of sovereign nations. The absence of an international legislature makes law-making a little cumbersome and time-consuming, but that is an inevitable consequence of sovereignty.

> There is certainly no shortage of international laws that touch on many aspects of our lives.

Notwithstanding these differences and difficulties, there is certainly no shortage of international laws that touch on many aspects of our lives. These laws are universally respected and applied. There are the laws that control civil aviation over-flying national air space, laws relating to posts and telecommunications, the law of the sea and international trade. And, of course, the rapid growth of literally hundreds of treaties on international criminal law—drug trafficking, trafficking in people, extradition, refugees, war crimes

and terrorism. And more and more courts are being established to implement these laws—the Law of the Sea Tribunal, the Appellate Body of the World Trade Organization, the International Criminal Court, the ad hoc Tribunals for the former Yugoslavia and Rwanda, the mixed tribunals for Sierra Leone, Cambodia and Lebanon. Then there are regional courts such as the European Court of Justice, the European Court of Human Rights, the African Court of Justice and the African Union Court of Human and Peoples Rights, the Inter-American Court of Human Rights. And then there are too many sub-regional courts to mention.

There are opinions and orders coming from these courts in their hundreds. What is important is that the majority of them are honored—they are either complied with or enforced. The number of international and regional judges has grown exponentially. And I need

The first group of judges for the International Criminal Tribunal for the former Yugoslavia (ICTY) in The Hague, Netherlands, in June 1995. (Raphael Gaillarde/Gamma-Rapho via Getty Images.)

hardly add that the legal profession has responded to what has become a growth industry.

In this context, the absence of an international executive power can be troublesome. It makes the implementation of some international laws more difficult as their enforcement is subject to the goodwill and cooperation of governments. However, as the world contracts, governments recognize more frequently the importance of reciprocity with regard to international law and order. For this reason compliance and cooperation is growing.

Though Complex, International Justice Is Crucial

The rapid growth of international law has left little time for the consideration of the rule of law at this supranational level. Is the international judiciary truly independent? How are international judges appointed? Is there equality before the laws implemented by these courts? Is due process recognized and implemented in trials and hearings before these courts? Is there an independent international bar?

The report card to date is a mixed one. There is much work to be done on improving the method of appointing the judges of many of these courts. Merit and not political expediency should be the rule. Oftentimes it is not. In some of the courts the judges might well be independent, but a system of reappointment might well produce the fear of political expediency in some of their decisions. They are dependent on their government for reappointment and that is likely to affect the fact or at least the perception of an absence of independence. . . .

I would like to spend what time I have left to turn to the importance of international justice and its contribution to the international rule of law. The starting point is impunity for war criminals. It is clearly inconsistent with an international rule of law to grant impunity to those who commit international war crimes.

In South Africa, the former Apartheid leaders of a white minority claimed blanket amnesties as the price for giving up power. For obvious reasons they wanted impunity. It was more than sufficient, they could claim, with some justification, to expect them to hand over power to a black majority that had been oppressed by cruel racial oppression for almost 350 years. To expect them in addition to face Nuremberg style trials and face prison sentences was just too much to demand of them. They argued that there was no advantage in looking backward. There was too great and expensive an agenda in building a new democratic South Africa. They, of course, were well aware of those awful crimes that had been committed in the enforcement of the Apartheid laws. Some of them came to light in the investigations I conducted during the last three years of Apartheid.

> Fortunately, Nelson Mandela and his colleagues were not prepared to go the route of national amnesia.

Fortunately, Nelson Mandela and his colleagues were not prepared to go the route of national amnesia. They were not prepared to sweep those past violations under the rug. The victims of Apartheid demanded acknowledgement and our new leaders knew that there would be no peaceful transition without it. The result was the Truth and Reconciliation Commission and discrete amnesties in return for full confessions. The outcome was a huge outpouring of evidence from over 21,000 victims and applications for amnesty from over 7,000 who claimed they were perpetrators. That evidence established beyond any question, and to the embarrassment of most white South Africans, what happened during those dark and evil years. The result is that today South Africa has a single history of the serious and many human rights violations that were committed in those bad years. That augurs well for the future.

Two Leaders of the Bosnian Serbs

Karadzic Led a Serb Government

The president of the Bosnian Serbs, who was later charged with genocide by the United Nations war crimes tribunal, was educated as a psychiatrist and also wrote poetry and children's books. His studies included a year at Columbia University in New York City.

Before the Bosnia conflict began, Radovan Karadzic lived with his wife, son, and daughter in a multiethnic apartment building in Sarajevo. But then, in partnership with Serb president Slobodan Milosevic, Karadzic led the campaign to eradicate non-Serbs in Bosnia in the 1990s.

After the conflict ended and he was indicted, Karadzic went into hiding and was not captured until 2008. In custody prior to his trial, he told a reporter for the *Irish Examiner* in August 2009: "I carried out my duties with the best interest of the people in my heart."

Mladic Led the Serb Troops

The commander of the Bosnian Serb armed forces grew up in poverty and was admired by his troops for battlefield bravery.

Ratko Mladic directed the siege of Sarajevo, which lasted more than three years and claimed ten thousand lives. During that time, his twenty-two-year-old daughter Ana, who was a medical student, killed herself. She was reportedly distraught that a Serbian magazine portrayed her father as a murderer.

The next year Mladic ordered the massacre of eight thousand Muslim men and boys at Srebrenica, according to an indictment by the UN war crimes tribunal.

After the conflict, he lived an increasingly secretive life in Belgrade, Serbia's capital. The fact that he remained uncaptured and untried for war crimes became controversial. The *New York Times* reported in October 2010 that Mladic had long been protected by armed men with military training.

A Hunt for Truth Succeeds

A comparable outcome has resulted from the work of the United Nations ad hoc criminal tribunal for the former Yugoslavia. The testimony of hundreds of witnesses has laid bare the crimes that accompanied terrible wars of the early 1990s and the egregious war crimes committed against thousands of innocent children, women and men. There, too, the testimony of hundreds of witnesses put an end to the false denials that were so common in the aftermath of the criminality of evil leaders and their followers. Allow me to give you just one illustration. A member of the Bosnian Serb Army, Drazan Erdemovic, was one of the members of an assassination squad outside Srebrenica in July 1995. The massacre of over 8,000 civilians, men and boys, was strenuously denied by the Bosnian Serb Army. Then, in early 1996, for personal reasons, Erdemovic decided to tell his story to an American TV network, ABC. A journalist and cameraman flew to Serbia and interviewed him some kilometers outside Belgrade. He admitted to having shot more than 70 innocent civilians. He had objected to this role but his own life and those of his family were threatened by his commander and he proceeded with his ghastly role under that duress. He also gave the journalist a map of the precise location of the mass grave of those who were murdered.

The journalist fortunately left the map at the US Embassy in Belgrade and then called her London office to say she was on her way back that evening with the video tape. She was met at the Belgrade Airport by Serb Security Police who confiscated the video film.

On arrival in London, the journalist called me in quite an emotional state. She understandably felt that she had placed the life of Erdemovic in jeopardy and asked whether I could assist in any way. I decided that the widest publicity to the event was the best way to protect his life and I obtained an order from the Tribunal requesting the Serb Government to transfer Erdemovic to The Hague as a potential defendant and witness to the events in Srebrenica. Fortunately for the Tribunal, Erdemovic was not a Serb national and in order to garner financial assistance from the United States, Milosevic, to our great surprise, decided to accede to the request and Erdemovic was flown to The Hague. The Serb Army continued to deny the massacre and ascribed the evidence of Erdemovic to US propaganda against Serbia.

We recovered the map the journalist had left at the US Embassy in Belgrade and that enabled us to send the coordinates to the United States Government. They sent us satellite photographs of the site of the massacre and they fully corroborated the version of Erdemovic. We had the grave exhumed and the forensic evidence provided further crucial corroboration of the evidence—the bodies were those of men and boys who had died in about the middle of 1995. All had their hands tied behind their backs and the cause of death was a single bullet wound to the head. That evidence effectively put an end to the false denials. It enabled the Tribunal to convict Erdemovic of crimes against humanity and formed the basis of subsequent findings of genocide against Bosnian Serb leaders. Also, in February 2007, the International Court of Justice followed the Tribunal in finding that Serbia could have prevented what it also held was genocide committed at Srebrenica. I need hardly tell you how important those events were for many thousands of members of the families of those murdered in the middle of 1995 outside Srebrenica. It brought them acknowledgement and closure. It allowed a large number of them to begin their own healing process. And, of course, it put an end to the false denials that had accompanied the massacre. And, only one week ago the trial of Radovan Karadzic began in The Hague. One of the charges against him is the genocide committed at Srebrenica. The evidence of Erdemovic will loom large at that trial.

In Rwanda, the genocide that resulted in the deaths of some 800,000 innocent people was described in minute detail in the evidence placed before the United Nations International Criminal Tribunal for Rwanda. There were also denials and they have stopped in light of the evidence again of hundreds of witnesses.

Absent these forms of justice—whether truth and reconciliation commissions or prosecutions before international criminal courts—the societies in question would today be very different and, I would suggest, they would be more violent societies. South Africans can now rebuild my country in the knowledge that white South Africans have a debt to pay for what was done by them or in their names. Although an enduring peace has not come to the states of the former Yugoslavia, the cannons have been silent for some fourteen years. And, hopefully, cycles of violence have been stopped in Rwanda.

> In both the former Yugoslavia and Rwanda . . . it was primarily the perpetrators who cast doubt on the processes of truth-making.

I have no doubt that some form of justice is essential in the Middle East if there is to be an enduring peace there.

In both the former Yugoslavia and Rwanda, attacks were made on the institutions designed to bring the truth to light. It was primarily the perpetrators who cast doubt on the processes of truth-making. They did what they could to prevent their establishment and having been established from fulfilling their mandates. That they did not succeed was due in no small measure to the role of [former US assistant secretary of state for democracy, human rights and labor] John Shattuck. . . . It was through his efforts and those of the Ambassador [Madeleine] Albright that there is now a permanent International Criminal Court up and hard at work in The Hague. It now has the support of 110 nations including that of every member of the European Union. Its jurisdiction is making itself felt by many in capitals of countries accused of committing serious war crimes. It is the living proof that we no longer live in an age of impunity for war criminals.

The United States' Strategy Was Correct for Bosnia, and for the Future

Richard Holbrooke

In the following selection, an American diplomat asserts that after any large conflict overseas there is an American tendency to pull back, and then crises arise that deserve new involvement. The conflict in Bosnia was an example of late but necessary US participation. Countering the absolute evil of some—by far not all—Serbs and then ensuring peace were indeed in US interests, he says, and similar difficult choices await in the future. Richard Holbrooke began a long career as a US diplomat in 1962 in Vietnam. An author, editor, investment bank executive, and twice assistant secretary of state, Holbrooke was the chief architect of the Dayton peace agreement, which ended the Bosnian conflict.

SOURCE. Richard Holbrooke, "America, Europe, and Bosnia," *To End a War*. New York: Random House, 1998, pp. 364–369. Copyright © 1998 by Richard Holbrooke; Maps copyright © 1998 by David Lindroth, Inc. Used by permission of Random House, Inc.

Even with the Cold War over, what happens in Europe still matters to the United States. This is not self-evident to most Americans, who thought the need for direct American involvement in Europe—and for that matter, most of the rest of the world—would end or decline sharply with the fall of communism.

But American involvement in Europe is not limited to crusades against fascism or communism. Deeper, less tangible factors tie the two continents together. Three times earlier in this century, the United States engaged deeply on the European continent: in World War I, in World War II, and in the Cold War. After each of the first two involvements, the United States withdrew, or began to withdraw, from the continent: in 1919–20, when it decided not to join the international institution President [Woodrow] Wilson had helped create, and in 1945–47. After World War II, America's leaders recognized that the country's national interests required a continued involvement in Europe, as well as in Asia. But when their initial policy, based on the effectiveness of the United Nations, failed because it required the positive participation of the Soviet Union, the [Harry S.] Truman Administration quickly recognized its initial misjudgment of Moscow and entered into the century's third American engagement in Europe, one that led to the collapse of the Soviet Union at the end of 1991.

Then, after fifty years of costly involvement in Europe, Americans hoped to focus on domestic priorities and disengage as much as possible from international commitments. Although understandable, this hope was unrealistic. Well before the Bosnia negotiations began, I argued that "an unstable Europe would still threaten essential security interests of the United States." But, with the disappearance of the Soviet Union, most Americans

> With the disappearance of the Soviet Union . . . there was no clear and present threat to the Western democracies.

no longer believed this. There was no clear and present threat to the Western democracies, no Hitler or Stalin. Moreover, for the first time since 1917, Russia and its former republics had to be incorporated into Europe's security structure rather than excluded from it. This new European security structure could not be built while part of it, the former Yugoslavia, was in flames. Settling Bosnia was necessary, although not sufficient, for true stability and long-term economic growth in Europe.

The policies of the last half century produced unparalleled peace and prosperity for half a century—but for only half a continent. With the war over in Bosnia, building a new European security architecture that included both the United States and Russia could finally proceed. NATO, long the private preserve of the nations on one side of the Iron Curtain, could gradually open its doors to qualified Central European nations—in a manner that neither threatened Russia nor weakened the alliance. Meanwhile, a new role for Russia, Ukraine, and the other parts of the former Soviet Union was being defined through new agreements like the Founding Act, which created a formal relationship between Russia and NATO yet did not give Russia a veto power over NATO activities. Other existing institutions, like the Organization for Security and Cooperation in Europe (OSCE), were strengthened and expanded.

Institutional and Structural Barriers

The great architect of European unity, Jean Monnet, once observed, "Nothing is possible without men, but nothing is lasting without institutions." It has become commonplace to observe that achieving Monnet's vision is far more difficult in the absence of the unifying effect of a common adversary. But we should not wax nostalgic for the Cold War. It is now institutional and structural problems that inhibit progress on both sides of the Atlantic.

President of Bosnia Alija Izetbegovic (left) shakes hands with Serbian president Slobodan Milosevic as Franjo Tudjman, president of Croatia, watches as peace negotiations begin in Dayton, Ohio, in 1995. (AP Photo/Joe Marquette, pool.)

The United States has survived divided government between the Executive Branch and the Congress for much of the last two decades. But a bloated bureaucratic system and a protracted struggle between the two branches have eroded much of Washington's capacity for decisive action in foreign affairs and reduced our presence just as our range of interests has increased. The United States continues to reduce the resources committed to international affairs even as vast parts of the globe—the former Soviet bloc, China—and new issues that once lay outside its area of direct involvement now take on new importance and require American attention. One cannot have a global economic policy without a political and strategic vision to accompany it, as the 1997–98 economic crisis in East Asia has shown.

If the search for a process that can produce coherent policies is difficult in Washington, it seems to be virtually impossible in the new Europe. [Swedish foreign afairs minister] Carl Bildt has made a useful observation: the United States, he points out, has to harmonize "institutional views" while Europe has to coordinate "national views." Bildt, who saw the two systems from a unique vantage point, observed:

> In Washington everything has to be formulated and shaped in a continuous compromise between the State Department, the Defense Department, the Treasury, intelligence agencies, and purely domestic factors. The rivalry between these various interests sometimes runs very deep. A great deal of blood can be spilt in the course of inter-agency debates in Washington. *But when this apparatus finally decides on a policy, the United States then has the resources to implement its policy which is almost completely lacking in Europe* [emphasis added].

Strategic Interests and Human Rights Combine

Advocates of realpolitik [practical politics], like three of its most famous American practitioners, Richard Nixon, Henry Kissinger, and George Kennan, have long argued that American advocacy of human rights conflicted with America's true national security interests, amounted to interference in the internal affairs of other nations, and weakened the nation's strategic and commercial interests. In his most recent book, *Diplomacy*, Kissinger portrayed American foreign policy as a constant struggle between realism, symbolized by Theodore Roosevelt, and idealism, as epitomized by Woodrow Wilson. Kissinger, who strongly favored TR, wrote, "The American experience has encouraged the belief that America, alone among the nations of the world, is impervious and that it can prevail by the example of its virtues and good works. In the post-Cold War world, such an attitude would turn innocence into self-indulgence."

Under Presidents [Richard] Nixon, [Gerald] Ford, and [George H.W.] Bush, such "realist" theories were in the ascendancy. (The [Jimmy] Carter Administration and the [Ronald] Reagan Administration, after the forced departure of Secretary of State Al Haig, took much more assertive positions on human rights.) But based on personal experiences in the late 1970s with authoritarian leaders like Ferdinand Marcos of the Philippines and Park Chung Hee of South Korea—both of whose corrupt strongman regimes were peacefully replaced by democracies—I came to the conclusion that the choice between "realists" and "idealists" was a false one: in the long run, our strategic interests and human rights supported and reinforced each other, and could be advanced at the same time. In short, American foreign policy needed to embrace both Theodore Roosevelt and Woodrow Wilson. These thoughts were never far from my mind as we searched for a way to end the [Bosnian] war.

> Our strategic interests and human rights supported and reinforced each other, and could be advanced at the same time.

Throughout the negotiations, I thought often of the refugees I had visited in 1992: how they knew many of the men who had killed and raped their families; how some of the killers had been their co-workers for twenty years; and how they had hardly been aware of ethnic hatred until 1990. Some people offered what had happened during World War II as proof that ethnic hatred was in the Yugoslav bloodstream. But the bloodbath and fighting of 1941–45 were a product of the larger struggle and genocide Hitler had unleashed. The rest of Europe found a path to peace and reconciliation, but Yugoslavia suffered a bad case of arrested development under communism. Then demagogic and criminal leaders seized power.

The killers were driven by ethnic prejudice rekindled by ultranationalists and demagogues. How could adults do such things to their neighbors and former classmates? After a while, the search for explanations failed. One simply had to recognize that there was true evil in the world.

> One simply had to recognize that there was true evil in the world.

The full ferocity of that evil so stunned most Europeans and Americans that they could not at first comprehend it. Then, as Carl Jung had warned, they did not know "what to pit against it." There was confusion over whom to blame, and disputes about what was happening; this increased as the war continued, since atrocities were committed by members of all three ethnic groups. But although Croats and Muslims were also guilty of atrocities, the Bosnian Serbs remained the primary perpetrators of the actions that made the phrase "ethnic cleansing" a part of the English language.

It was easy to conclude, as [US secretary of state Lawrence] Eagleburger did, that nothing could be done by outsiders. Or that Serbs were inherently evil. Such judgments allowed people to justify their own inaction. But drawing either inference would be to share the fundamental mistake of the people of the Balkans themselves, imputing to an entire ethnic group the attributes of its worst elements. For more than fifty years people had debated the degree to which the entire German people shared culpability for the Holocaust, and now a similar question arose: was the entire Serb "nation" responsible for the actions of its leaders and their murderous followers?

I often received letters, primarily from Serbs or Serbian Americans, charging that my remarks, or those of other American officials, lumped all Serbs together with a few indicted war criminals. This was a fair criticism of comments that could not always be precise. In fact, the majority of Serbs in the former Yugoslavia were ordinary people who did not kill anyone, although, like many "good Germans" during the Third Reich, a large number remained silent or passive in the face of something they admitted later they knew was wrong. But others were courageous opponents of the fires that raged across their land, and some even fought on the Muslim side. One of contemporary Europe's great visionaries, Czech President Vaclav Havel, addressed this issue in an eloquent essay:

> I consider it an offense against the Serbian people and betrayal of the civic notion of society when evil is identified with Serbian nationality. But I find it equally misguided when evil is not defined at all, for fear of hurting Serbian feelings. All peoples have their Karadžićs and Mladićs, either real or potential. If such men—as the result of a mix of historical, social, and cultural circumstances—gain greater influence than they have in other parts of the world, it does not mean that they come from a criminal people. . . . [This] is a conflict of principles, not of nationalities. . . . In other words, let us beware of attempts to lay the blame for evil on whole peoples. That would be tantamount to adopting the ideology of the ethnic fanatics.

The Bosnian Conflict Was Not Unique

After Dayton we came full circle, back to an uncertainty about how much to invest in Bosnia. Having put American prestige on the line in 1995 to end the war, the United States and its allies were uncertain in 1996 and early 1997 about how hard to try to make Dayton work. The result was halfhearted implementation that led critics and cynics to call for scaled-back objectives in Bosnia. Failure to squash the separatist Serb movement immediately after Dayton, when it lay in disarray, seemed to some to prove that partition was inevitable. Such preemptive defeatism could have led to the permanent partition of Bosnia, followed by more refugees and more fighting. The best course remained vigorous enforcement of the Dayton agreement. At the end of 1997, President [Bill] Clinton's decision to remove the time limit for U.S. troops dramatically enhanced the chance of success. In 1998 the main constraint was no longer the separatists of Pale, who were beaten, corrupt, and in disarray. Success was within sight, but it would take hard work and a firm commitment from the leaders of the international community—and time.

> America and its allies often seem too willing to ignore problems outside their heartland.

The circumstances that led to the collapse of Yugoslavia and the war in Bosnia were so extraordinary that it is difficult to conceive of their recurrence. Yet if history teaches us one thing, it is that history is unpredictable. There will be other Bosnias in our lives, different in every detail but similar in one overriding manner: they will originate in distant and ill-understood places, explode with little warning, and present the rest of the world with difficult choices—choices between risky involvement and potentially costly neglect. But if during the Cold War Washington sometimes seemed too ready to intervene, today America and its allies often seem too willing to ignore problems outside their heartland.

There will be other Bosnias in our lives—areas where early outside involvement can be decisive, and American leadership will be required. The world's richest nation, one that presumes to great moral authority, cannot simply make worthy appeals to conscience and call on others to carry the burden. The world will look to Washington for more than rhetoric the next time we face a challenge to peace.

CHAPTER 3

Personal Narratives

Each Day Became Worse for a Girl in Sarajevo

Zlata Filipović

A girl in Sarajevo, Bosnia's main city, began keeping a diary in September 1991, a few months before the city came under siege. She lived in a spacious, elegant apartment, with relatives and friends nearby. Then, from the hills above, artillery shells began exploding in the city. In the following excerpt from her diary, Filipović, then thirteen years old, describes the family's struggle for survival. She calls her diary "Mimmy." Zlata Filipović escaped from Sarajevo, with her parents, on December 23, 1993. They lived in Paris for less than two years and then moved to Ireland. After college, she worked as a translator and editor.

Photo on previous page: The names of more than 80,000 victims of the Srebrenica massacre are engraved on the wall of the Memorial Center and Cemetery at Potocari, Bosnia. (**AP Photo/Amel Emric.**)

SOURCE. Zlata Filipović, "Wednesday, May 27, 1992," *Zlata's Diary: A Child's Life in Sarajevo*, translated by Christina Pribichevich-Zoric. New York: Viking Penguin, 1994. Copyright © 1994 Editions Robert Laffont/Fixot. Used by permission of Viking Penguin, a division of Penguin Group (USA) Inc.

Wednesday, May 27, 1992
Dear Mimmy,
SLAUGHTER! MASSACRE! HORROR! CRIME!
BLOOD! SCREAMS! TEARS! DESPAIR!
That's what Vaso Miškin Street looks like today. Two
shells exploded in the street and one in the market.
Mommy was nearby at the time. She ran to Grandma and
Granddad's. Daddy and I were beside ourselves because
she hadn't come home. I saw some of it on TV but I still
can't believe what I actually saw. It's unbelievable. I've
got a lump in my throat and a knot in my tummy. HOR-
RIBLE. They're taking the wounded to the hospital. It's a
madhouse. We kept going to the window hoping to see
Mommy, but she wasn't back. They released a list of the
dead and wounded. Daddy and I were tearing our hair
out. We didn't know what had happened to her. Was she
alive? At 4:00, Daddy decided to go and check the hospital. He got dressed, and I got ready to go to the Bobars',
so as not to stay at home alone. I looked out the window
one more time and . . . I SAW MOMMY RUNNING
ACROSS THE BRIDGE. As she came into the house she
started shaking and crying. Through her tears she told
us how she had seen dismembered bodies. All the neighbors came because they had been afraid for her. Thank
God, Mommy is with us. Thank God.
A HORRIBLE DAY. UNFORGETTABLE.
HORRIBLE! HORRIBLE!
Your Zlata

Thursday, May 28, 1992
Dear Mimmy,
It started at around 10:00. First we went to Neda's. I
put Saša to sleep and left the bedroom. I looked toward
the bathroom, and then . . . BOOM. The window in the
bathroom shattered into pieces and I was alone in the
hall and saw it all. I began to cry hysterically. Then we
went down into the cellar. When things calmed down we

went up to Neda's and spent the night there. Today in Vaso Miškin Street people signed the book of mourning and laid flowers. They renamed the street and now it's called the Street of Anti-Fascist Resistance.

Zlata

> Two women were giving birth . . . Out of the flames, new lives are born.

Friday, May 29, 1992
Dear Mimmy,
I'm at Neda's. The result of last night's fascism is broken glass in Daddy's office and at the Bobars' shattered windows. A shell fell on the house across the way, and I can't even tell you how many fell nearby. The whole town was in flames.

Your Zlata

Saturday, May 30, 1992
Dear Mimmy,
The City Maternity Hospital has burned down. I was born there. Hundreds of thousands of new babies, new residents of Sarajevo, won't have the luck to be born in this maternity hospital now. It was new. The fire devoured everything. The mothers and babies were saved. When the fire broke out two women were giving birth. The babies are alive. God, people get killed here, they die here, they disappear, things go up in flames here, and out of the flames, new lives are born.

Your Zlata

Monday, June 1, 1992
Dear Mimmy,
Today is Maja's birthday. She's eighteen. She's an adult now. She's a grown-up. It's an important day in her life, but, what can you do, she's celebrating it in wartime. We all did our best to make this day special for her, but she was sad and moody. Why did this war have to ruin everything for

her? Maja isn't even having her senior prom, or an evening gown. All there is here is war, war and more war.

Fortunately, there wasn't too much shooting, so we could sit in peace. Auntie Boda made a special lunch (how special can it be in wartime???). Mommy used the last walnuts in the house to make a cake (Maja and her eighteen years deserve it). We gave her a necklace and bracelet made of Ohrid pearls. She got a lot of valuable presents made of gold. Well, you're only eighteen once in your life. Happy birthday to you Maja on this big day, may all your other birthdays be celebrated in peace.

Zlata

> It started to thunder again. No, not the weather, the shells.

Friday, June 5, 1992

Dear Mimmy,

There's been no electricity for quite some time and we keep thinking about the food in the freezer. There's not much left as it is. It would be a pity for all of it to go bad. There's meat and vegetables and fruit. How can we save it?

Daddy found an old wood-burning stove in the attic. It's so old it looks funny. In the cellar we found some wood, put the stove outside in the yard, lit it and are trying to save the food from the refrigerator. We cooked everything, and joining forces with the Bobars, enjoyed ourselves. There was veal and chicken, squid, cherry strudel, meat and potato pies. All sorts of things. It's a pity, though, that we had to eat everything so quickly. We even over-ate. WE HAD A MEAT STROKE.

We washed down our refrigerators and freezers. Who knows when we'll be able to cook like this again. Food is becoming a big problem in Sarajevo. There's nothing to buy, and even cigarettes and coffee are becoming a problem for grown-ups. The last reserves are being used up. God, are we going to go hungry to boot???

Zlata

Wednesday, June 10, 1992

Dear Mimmy,

At about eleven o'clock last night it started to thunder again. No, not the weather, the shells. We ran over to Nedo's. I fell asleep there, but Mommy and Daddy went back home.

There's no electricity. We're cooking on the wood stove in the yard. Everybody is. The whole neighborhood. What luck to have this old stove.

Daddy and Žika keep fiddling with the radio, listening to the news. They found RFI (Radio France Internationale) in our language. That's at nine o'clock in the evening and they listen to it regularly. Bojana and I usually play cards, word games or draw something.

Love,

Zlata

Sunday, June 14, 1992

Dear Mimmy,

There's still no electricity, so we're still cooking on the stove in the yard. Around 2:00, when we were doing something around the stove, a shell fell on the opposite corner of the street, destroying Zoka's wonderful jewelry shop. We ran straight to the cellar, waiting for the barrage. Luckily there was only that one shell, so we went back at around 4:00.

Your Zlata

Tuesday, June 16, 1992

Dear Mimmy,

Our windows are broken. All of them except the ones in my room. That's the result of the revolting shell that fell again on Zoka's jewelry shop, across the way from us. I was alone in the house at the time. Mommy and Daddy were down in the yard, getting lunch ready, and I had gone upstairs to set the table. Suddenly I heard a terrible bang and glass breaking. I was terrified and ran toward the hall. That same moment, Mommy and Daddy were at the door. Out of breath, worried, sweating and pale they hugged me and we ran to the cellar, because the shells usually come one after the other. When I realized what had happened, I started to cry and shake. Everybody tried to calm me down, but I was very upset. I barely managed to pull myself together.

We returned to the apartment to find the rooms full of glass and the windows broken. We cleared away the glass and put plastic sheeting over the windows. We had had a close shave with that shell and shrapnel. I picked up a piece of shrapnel and the tail end of a grenade, put them in a box and thanked God I had been in the kitchen, because I could have been hit . . . HORRIBLE! I don't know how often I've written that word. HORRIBLE. We've had too much horror. The days here are full of horror. Maybe we in Sarajevo could rename the day and call it horror, because that's really what it's like.

Love,
Zlata

Thursday, June 18, 1992
Dear Mimmy,

Today we heard some more sad, sad news. Our country house in Crnotina, a tower that's about 150 years old, has burned down. Like the post office, it disappeared in the flames. I loved it so much. We spent last summer there. I had a wonderful time. I always looked forward to going there. We had redone it so nicely, bought new furniture, new rugs, put in new windows, given it all our love and warmth, and its beauty was our reward. It lived through so many wars, so many years and now it's gone. It has burned down to the ground. Our neighbors Žiga, Meho and Bečir were killed. That's even sadder. Vildana's house also burned

> I keep asking why? What for? Who's to blame? I ask, but there's no answer.

down. All the houses burned down. Lots of people were killed. It's terribly sad news.

I keep asking why? What for? Who's to blame? I ask, but there's no answer. All I know is that we are living in misery. Yes, I know, politics is to blame for it all. I said I wasn't interested in politics, but in order to find out the answer I have to know something about it. They tell me only a few things. I'll probably find out and understand much more one day. Mommy and Daddy don't discuss politics with me. They probably think I'm too young or maybe they themselves don't know anything. They just keep telling me: This will pass—"it has to pass"????????

Your Zlata

Saturday, June 20, 1992
Dear Mimmy,

Auntie Radmila (Mommy's friend from work) came today. She came from Vojničko polje (a new housing complex). Her apartment has been completely destroyed. Wiped out in the shelling. Everything in it has been destroyed. All that's left is a useless pile of furniture, clothes, pictures and all the other things that go into an apartment. She's sad, because her daughters Sunčica and Mirna aren't there (they're in Zagreb), but she's glad they didn't have to live through the hell of Vojničko polje. Today we heard that Narmin Tulič, the actor at the Experimental Theater, lost both his legs. Awful! Awful! Awful!

Saša went to stay with his grandmother. But he'll probably be coming back.

Your Zlata

Monday, June 22, 1992
Dear Mimmy,

More blood on the streets of Sarajevo. Another massacre. In Tito Street. Three people killed, thirty-five wounded. Shells fell on Radič, Miss Irbin and Šenoa streets. About fifteen people were killed in the three streets. I'm worried that something may have happened to Marina's, Marijana's or Ivana's parents.

These people just go on killing. MURDERS! I pity them for being so very, very stupid, so servile, for humiliating themselves so much in front of certain people. Terrible!!!!!!

Your Zlata

Moral Bravery Persists Amid the Desperation for Survival

Zlatko Dizdarevic

During the siege of Sarajevo, a local newspaper editor records how residents try to live with honor and sanity in a situation that becomes more and more humiliating and crazed. Each day could be the last for each of the people about whom he writes—and for himself. Yet he finds modest and admirable acts of humanity amid destruction. In such a time and place, Dizdarevic writes, the details of life take on great importance. Zlatko Dizdarevic was an editor for *Oslobodenje*, the last daily newspaper to operate in Bosnia during the conflict. He survived the Sarajevo siege and continued to write afterward.

SOURCE. Zlatko Dizdarevic, "Sarajevo Stories," *Bulletin of the Atomic Scientists*, v. 50, no. 2, March–April, 1994, pp. 30–37. Used by permission.

May 17, 1992: Yesterday, in the midst of the chaos of war, a small news item arrived, so small it was almost imperceptible, announcing that the school year 1991–1992 is now over, that the students' grades will be the same as they were on the first day of the war, while failing grades have been raised by one point.

My friend Boro, who with other colleagues stays around the clock at the offices of Oslobodenje in order to protect and produce the paper, received the news from his daughter, whom the war has prevented from finishing her first school year. On the day classes were canceled, all her grades were five out of five, and thus she finished this truncated year with perfect grades. Do you know what she asked for, timidly and in a near-whisper to celebrate this success? "Papa, since I've done so well, could you buy me an ice cream cone?"

Boro is a man of the world, competent and successful. Before she started school, Lana could have had all the ice cream she wanted. In those days, before the destruction and the tears, Lana would have been rewarded for her grades with whatever Boro could have afforded to buy her. Today, even in her great little world, she has understood the meaning of the sights that surround her, she has assimilated the message of values circumscribed by hunger and thirst, poverty, grief, and loss. And in her great little world, that ice cream has become a dream that can only be hoped for.

The Hospital Is a Blasted Refuge

July 12, 1992: A routine two-hour visit to the Kosevo Hospital sums up the experience of the war in Sarajevo. Thousands of individual dramas are condensed into one desperate convulsion in an attempt to survive; then, after that, who knows?

Last night the orthopedic ward was under fire. A shell crashed through six rooms, leaving devastation in its wake. Scattered in the corners of the rooms lie abandoned crutches, which the patients had been clutching at like straws, in the hope that one day they could walk again. Overturned beds, blood, cement. . . . If he survives, Beslija Jazmir, a soldier from the front, will remember his fractured femur as an insignificant episode compared to the stomach wounds he received here last night. On the outside wall of the building, the shell's entry hole is surprisingly small, not crater-shaped at all; once inside, piercing one wall after another, the shell caused increasing damage, and sought out the same unlucky ones who had already been wounded in the bloody episode of Vasa Miskin Street. Death came for them a second time. . . .

> "The shell . . . sought out the same unlucky ones who had already been wounded."

But the story of the hospital is also the story of the children on the second floor of the orthopedic ward, among whom there are those who have had an arm or a leg amputated and are already showing a subconscious desire to prove themselves faster and more agile on their crutches than others. On the surface they seem in good spirits, and extraordinarily willing and able to tell you how, where, and why they became forever different from other children in the world. But they're already fighting their personal battles with sleepless nights and the emotional traumas they carry like a brand displaying their difference from others. One of them had been carrying ammunition to Trebevic. (Whose idea was that, and why?) Another had simply been playing in the wrong place, providing a target for a sniper. A third had been standing too close to a window.

In the hallway of the ward where these children begin their new lives as mutilated, amputated, permanently handicapped people, one may see vestiges of another time, remnants of other habits: large posters of the Pink Panther, Asterix the Gaul, and Donald Duck. Who in this clinic today, without a leg or a hand, wonders who the Pink Panther is, where that Duck is, or where Asterix comes from? But they will know, for the rest of their lives, who Dr. Karadzic is, they will learn about the monster Mladic, and Ostajic the criminal, and Milosevic, Cosic, Bulatovic, and the rest. . . . They will also know who we are, we who didn't know early enough how to protect their childhood, their legs or their hands. And they will also know what to think of a world that mumbles on about justice, order, and truth, of law, responsibility, and continuity.

Unity Surfaces in the Lion Cemetery

July 18, 1992: It's 2:00 P.M., and no one has been killed yet. It is a strange, torrid July afternoon. Because no one has been killed yet, because the firing is distant, it has been possible to bury those who were killed yesterday and the day before, as well as those whose corpses have lain for days in the dark and cold of hospital rooms serving as morgues. Processions of silent, exhausted, anxious people have made their way to the old Lion Cemetery, which has been reopened by a special decree from the municipal authorities.

Located between a shaded avenue that leads to Kosevo Stadium and a quiet street next to the Trauma Center, this cemetery has not seen many visitors lately. It is named after a monumental sculpture of a lion with a royal mane. Now it has become the only meeting place for Sarajevans who don't have any other occasion for gathering in large numbers in the same place.

Slowly at first, then more rapidly every day, a yellow wave of freshly turned soil replaces what was an untended lawn under the lion's paws. This wave spreads in all directions and devours parts of the cemetery that had already been sold for other uses. Two, three, 10, 15 burials a day is the Sarajevan rhythm of passage from life to death.

All the many years of life in Sarajevo, and for Sarajevo, can be seen in the shade of the Lion's Graveyard, as revealing as the palm of your hand. Sarajevo is really just a small town; it has great soul, and everyone here knows everyone else. These folk are the only ones buried here, beside the concrete lion, whose mane had long been chewed. But those who, for now, have found their resting place in the grass courtyards of Dobrinja, and in other places where the dead could not be carried out for a decent funeral, one day they will be here. The Lion's graves are the final resting places for those who are truly of Sarajevo, who refused to leave, and so will remain here forever.

It is astonishing to note that you recognize practically all the names on the hundreds and hundreds of inscriptions, even though some have faded; it is stupefying to see the names of people you had met only days before, smiling and convinced that you would meet again in the future. Then you realize that death in this city comes silently, unannounced, leaving not ever, the minimal space necessary for the farewell that befits us.

> "We loved the same life . . . we dug ourselves the same grave."

Under the dense foliage of the cemetery trees, you find the names of people you grew up with and knew in high school, names of others with whom you dreamed of your first journeys abroad, great journeys to happiness, to the infinite. We recognize the names of those with whom we lost touch, and only now, here, do we understand that we've always been members of the same Sarajevo band, that we loved the same life, that we dug ourselves the same grave because we didn't know how, or didn't want, to defy the hicks from the woods when we should have. We just kept telling jokes at their expense while they came down from the hills, dragging one after another, hating us because we knew about soap and water, about washing our feet and wearing clean socks.

So we congregate here today below the Lion, the lucky ones who are still standing and those of our gang who found themselves at the wrong place at the wrong time, and now lie here side by side.

A Woman Who Did Not Want to Beg

August 8, 1992: Our story, I'm afraid, is totally unreal. Sometimes I tell myself that people outside who don't know what is happening here must think that we're insane. All they need to do to get that impression from a distance is follow the people and events of Sarajevo for a little while. We, obviously, don't see it like this, but that's because we're lost in our daily troubles, and maybe also because we have so little energy left in the batteries that keep life running.

On Saturday, for instance, an elderly woman knocked on my door holding a note pad in her hand, explaining that she was collecting money for electricity. However, as I soon learned, it wasn't really a question of paying electricity bills, but only of collecting money. After exchanging only a few words it became clear to me what she was after. She said, politely and without the least embarrassment, "If you could pay for April, May, and June, that would be 3,000 dinars." Now, 3,000 dinars is nothing—it's 6 kilograms of bread, when you can get it—but it is a considerable sum for those who are destitute.

Thank God, now my friends are sharing the place with me and we have some means, since we sell our damned little newspaper, almost raising enough to cover our salaries. So we gave the woman 15,000 dinars, and she told us that would be enough for three more families who have nothing. She left satisfied.

Something similar happened on a bus that appeared out of nowhere, on a nonscheduled run along the city's main thoroughfare. The driver announced to us that he was going up to the television building and back. Right in front of us, a woman asked the conductor (who sat in

Food shortages in Sarajevo caused chaotic lines for such basic necessities as bread. (**AP Photo/David Brauchli.**)

his seat, in accordance with the regulations) how much the fare was. "If you have money, it's three dinars. If you don't, pay us when the war is over," the charming conductor told her.

We offered to pay the (as it turned out) penniless woman's fare, but the conductor wouldn't hear of it. "Please, it's out of the question. Our company, the municipal transportation enterprise, offers free rides to fellow citizens who have to get to work." Way to go! We had a nice ride, feeling less afraid than usual. Such a bus had to be immune to mortar shells and sniper bullets. Hopes of that sort are all we have left. Everything else is only ersatz existence.

Paranoid Guards Destroy the Phone System

August 16, 1992: The number of people you can get in touch with in this city shrinks every day. There are no cars; they're either wrecked, stolen, confiscated, or out of gas. The shelling and the snipers have made walking more dangerous than any hand-to-hand combat on the front lines. So driving and walking are out. And now they've started taking people's phones away. I don't know of anyone to whom this has happened who doesn't think life might become impossible here if conditions continue to be dictated by the heroes of our war offices.

> Local patriotic defense teams have mounted an implacable assault on Sarajevo's telephones.

Briefly: Someone has come to the conclusion that a Fifth Column is making use of the phone lines to inform the Chetniks how to correct their aim, where to shoot and whom to hit. Very conscientiously, local patriotic defense teams have mounted an implacable assault on Sarajevo's telephones. In an unparalleled demonstration of patriotism and officious zeal left over from the old days of the secret police, they have cut off the few phones that were genuine lifelines for entire streets and districts. Naturally, abandoned telephones found in some apartments have been put under strict surveillance by faithful members of the local "revolutionary guard." This will make it impossible for anyone to collaborate with the enemy. Or so they believe.

This mania has spread with pestilential rapidity from the quarters nearest the Chetnik lines to every other part of the city, imprisoned, encircled, and isolated as it is. Those of us who are left—still without water, electricity, radio, television, and now without the telephone—are nothing but sacrificial beasts, deprived of all rights except the right to loneliness, hunger, humiliation, and death.

In popular quarters, in dark basements, on the landings of apartment buildings these new Kapos are gathering to make decisions on the local level (against which there is no recourse) as to who gets to keep his phone and who has it cut off until some other decision has been reached.

But to what extent does the telephone really serve the Chetniks as a "means of transmission," when every little kid knows that signals of this type can be transmitted in a thousand different ways: from a pair of underpants on a line to curtains either open or shut. Not to mention the thousands of walkie-talkies in town, or even other more sophisticated methods, such as whispering. A more serious side to this story is posed by the fact that every little functionary is now convinced that he has the power to decide who has the right to use the telephone, who is potentially one of "ours," who potentially "theirs."

A Little Precious Food Arrives

November 3, 1992: It's a little nicer in town than a week or two ago. The so-called humanitarian aid got here yesterday. The lines in front of the distribution offices are endless, but people who have been perennially searching for food say that the aid is "super, it's never been better." "Super" means . . . per person, a few plastic bags with 3 centiliters (just about the size of a shot of brandy) of olive oil, 500 grams of flour, 200 grams of cheese, and—hang on to your hats—500 grams of potatoes. At the market potatoes cost 20 marks a kilo, just like onions, but 10 marks less than a liter of oil. You can also get a can of tomatoes per family ration card—in other words, for a whole "refuge apartment"—so that if you'd like to follow the Herzegovinian recipe for plain boiled rice, you can make it a little red.

Speaking of the market, there are a few other little improvements. Coal has arrived, at 50 marks a sack. A liter of fuel for lamps, to which you can add some salt, so it'll burn longer, goes for 10 marks. A pack of cigarettes, 3 marks. For those who prefer to price things in our currency, here are a few more prices: a pack of chewing gum, 600 dinars; a bag of candy, 1,000 dinars; a bottle of draft beer, 2,000 dinars. The average pensioner here pulls in 10,000 dinars/month, so you can figure it out for yourself.

> Will there be any more days, any more hope?

Of course, you can go for straight bartering, like in the times we seem to have again become part of. A liter of lamp fuel is worth 3 kilos of sugar, a can of anything gets you 10 kilos of flour. Or, as someone said recently, 10 Rembrandts for 2 liters of cooking oil. Here we know the true value of things.

Anxiety Grows; Trees Disappear

January 19, 1993: What wouldn't I give to know how all this will end! Do we still, after all that has happened, stand the slightest chance? Or is everything already lost? Is it futile to continue living in the hope that one day we will be vindicated, at the cost of our wounds? And will there be any more days, any more hope?

Today it is hard to fight back the tears in these eyes that have almost run dry, after the news of what has happened to an 11-year-old: Standing in line for water in the vicinity of Pivara (a brewery in town), both his father and mother were killed by sniper fire. As I write, half the personnel of the hospital is engaged in the battle to save the life of his sister, a girl of 17.

After the shooting, this boy started to fetch and pour water over the bodies of his dead parents. He didn't want to stop even when his sister, seriously wounded, told him: "Stop, Berin, stop, they're dead."

What's with this water that we, curiously robotic and near exhaustion, have been carrying in buckets for months? And what kind of power have we been waiting for these 40 days? What will we do with it, and it with us, if it comes back one day? Will it change anything for that woman who this morning slammed the door on a number of exhausted, thirsty people as soon as the water supply was restored to her building?

Who will replant—and when—the thousands of trees we have lost? Who will ever be able to sit in the shade of the old oak tree in the park down the street, which for days has been attacked with hatchets and all kinds of knives, like the Lilliputians hacking away at Gulliver, to no avail?

I hear that Disney movies have been banned in Belgrade. I am convinced that what they need there is more Disney. They should be able to see Disney movies, 10 times a day. Then, perhaps, Berin's parents would still be alive.

The Surreal Becomes Reality

August 18, 1993: Here in Sarajevo we have witnessed incredible things in the course of this war, but events of the past week have surpassed our worst nightmares. First of all, we were told to construct air-raid shelters because the bombardment, by the NATO air force, of Serb positions around Sarajevo was "imminent." Then, before more than a hundred journalists, an official U.N. spokesman calmly stated that Sarajevo was really not under siege, and that it was only the "warfare in central Bosnia" that created supply problems for our city. Later, the same sources informed us that the soldiers who had been besieging us for 15 months had retreated from the surrounding hills, and still later, that the "humanitarian blockade of the city will be lifted." At the end of this same week, we saw and heard the most incredible thing of all: a veritable hunt for wounded children in Sarajevo hospitals. Without notice, without a chance to say goodbye to their parents, these children were whisked off to Britain and elsewhere in a spectacular action to evacuate them with military aircraft.

This provided the crowning touch to the nightmare. True, there may be a perfectly logical reason for each of these actions. The adversarial game between the Americans and the Europeans, in which it's our heads that are at stake, had reached impressive proportions. In their effort to prevent the air strikes favored by the Americans, the Europeans once again showed great ingenuity. In order to demonstrate that there was no reason for such an action, they came up with an argument that must strike every Sarajevan as the sheerest fantasy: no need to panic, Sarajevo really isn't under siege.

However, in this suddenly "liberated" city, there now were over 160 foreign journalists who suddenly found themselves deprived of their anticipated show. The French and English Blue Helmets declared that since Sarajevo was not under siege, the air strikes would not take place after all, so the journalists, who had come here to cover the action, looked around for something else to report. Word of a seriously wounded young girl sent dozens of them on a chase for "their child," turning her evacuation from Sarajevo into a circus.

> Our city had been reduced to the status of a zoo.

The medical community of Sarajevo watched this chase, initiated by powerful television networks and newspapers, in astonishment. How was it possible to accomplish in a single day what had been unimaginable for so long? Where did all this money come from, this willingness to launch an operation a thousand times more expensive than the fuel the hospitals had been lacking for months? Owing to that lack of fuel, the most complicated surgical operations had been performed by candlelight. . . .

Why was it necessary to use military planes to transport these children, if Sarajevo no longer was under siege? And had it not been proclaimed that the wounded should be treated here, and not evacuated? True, in order to treat them here it would be necessary to improve conditions in Sarajevo, and the powers that be had not been helpful in that respect.

Once again, these events have shown us only what we already knew. The politics of the great powers and the politics of foreign television networks and newspapers allow them to do what they will with poor Sarajevo. Our city had been reduced to the status of a zoo. Personally, I am delighted to hear the news that Sarajevo isn't under siege. That means I can go wherever I want whenever I want; that I'm carrying 50 liters of water every day just to entertain myself; and that if I manage to have a meal only every other day, this is not because there is not food but because I don't want to eat any more than that. Furthermore, it reassures me to know that all the people killed in the last few days were not killed by shells fired from the hills; they simply committed suicide for their own pleasure.

At first we thought that no one understood Sarajevo at all. Then we believed that it was all a matter of great-power politics, and that we simply did not fit into that scheme. Today we know that the world is perverse, that it relishes our plight with a degree of sadism. The training of the circus animals has reached new heights. I only hope that the training don't lose control, and that the situation doesn't become too dangerous for the audience to watch.

The Contradictions of Bosnia Lead Toward Fear and Insanity

David Rieff

A seasoned American correspondent finds himself unprepared for what is happening in Bosnia. In that sense he is like the Bosnians themselves, he reveals in the following viewpoint. They simply could not imagine that a middle-class European lifestyle would include, for example, high-rise windows smashed by snipers' bullets. The writer finds himself drawn deeply into an always-frightening conflict bordered by global hypocrisy. David Rieff, journalist and author of eight books, is based in New York. He has covered conflicts in Africa, central Asia, and the Balkans.

To return to the life you led before you [lived through scenes of] slaughter and bloodshed, at least if you are a citizen of the rich world, is to choke on the cant and the complacency of everything

SOURCE. Reprinted with the permission of Simon & Schuster, Inc. from *Slaughterhouse: Bosnia and the Failure of the West* by David Rieff. Copyright © 1995 David Rieff.

that used to be familiar and pleasurable to you. You start to feel like an alien in the life you yourself have fashioned. In a sense, all writers, to greater or lesser degrees, must condition themselves to be professional outsiders. But for all my familiarity with that way of seeing things, traveling back and forth from a place like Sarajevo or Banja Luka to a place like Manhattan removed me from my friends and my past to a degree I had never dreamed possible. I felt not only is if I had returned from the land of the dead, but as if I too had become somehow posthumous.

And I believe that I am not alone in this. Even seasoned war correspondents have found it hard to recover from what they lived through in Bosnia. If now I write both in support of the Bosnian cause—this despite the fact that temperamentally I have always suspected causes and, in any case, I believe that cause has been lost—and in protest against the callous indifference, the shallow pessimism, and the hypocrisy that have surrounded the murder of Bosnia, I suspect that I am more surprised by my own stance than anyone. In a previous life, the life before Bosnia, I used to flatter myself that indignation was an emotion to which I was virtually immune. Just as I did not expect to end up in Bosnia in the first place, so I did not expect to feel that I would never recover from it.

> In all the time I spent in Bosnia, I cannot remember a single moment when I was not at least a little frightened.

This has nothing to do with feeling comfortable there, let alone imagining, as people often do when they fall in love with countries or causes, that I somehow "belonged." In all the time I spent in Bosnia, I cannot remember a single moment when I was not at least a little frightened, and I remember many moments when I was terrified. I was then, and I remain, intensely critical of the Bosnian government, in both its policies and its naïveté, and often bored and exasperated by the way the Bosnians talked with such a combination of self-absorption and lack of realism about themselves and the rest of the world. Nevertheless, it has seemed easier to be in Bosnia, however hopeless or exasperating things could seem there, than to listen to the way Bosnia was usually talked of, or, worse still, not talked of, ignored, in the West.

That one heard so little about Bosnia in countries like Germany and Italy that were so near was something I soon got used to. But the emblematic moment for me was when, a year into the slaughter, long after the beginning of the siege of Sarajevo, long after the Bosnian Serb forces had expelled from the valleys of eastern Bosnia most of their former majority of Muslim inhabitants, and long after the overwhelming majority of the mosques of northern Bosnia had been blown up, thus eliminating the traces of a European Islam that had existed in the region for five centuries, President [Bill] Clinton presided over the opening of the Holocaust Museum in Washington, D.C. It was a blustery day, replete with clenched jaws, somber clothes, and flights of rhetorical purposefulness. The President of Croatia, Franjo Tudjman, who at one time expressed skepticism about the very existence of the Holocaust, was in the audience. So were many of its survivors, including Elie Wiesel, who, to his credit, reproached Clinton for America's Bosnia policy. For his part, the President wanted to confine the conversation to generalities. He did have one suggestion, though. So that the genocide that befell European Jewry during the Nazi period never take place again, Bill Clinton insisted, extraordinary vigilance was necessary. "We must deploy memory," he said.

That President Clinton could speak of memory as if it were something like a moral antiballistic missile system was the least of it. The real moral solecism was to speak

optimistically about the future when, as he knew perfectly well, and Wiesel would soon remind him from the
podium, another genocide was taking place in Europe.
The Bosnian genocide was not identical to what had
happened to the Jews, any more than the extermination
of the European Jewry had been identical to the genocide
of the Armenians in 1915. Genocide had been the goad
behind the adoption of such principles of post-World
War II international order as the Four Geneva Conventions, the Genocide Convention of 1949, and, above all,
the United Nations Charter. And these laws were being
systematically violated in Bosnia.

Clinton's Statement Ignored Reality

The siege of Sarajevo was itself a war crime. On the
battlefield, usually it was rarer to find instances where
war crimes *had not* been committed than where they
had. And, of course, ethnic cleansing was not just a war
crime, it was genocide, pure and simple. To utter words
like "Never again," as Clinton did at the opening of the
Holocaust Museum, was to take vacuity over the border
into obscenity as long as the genocide in Bosnia was
going on and Clinton was doing nothing to stop it. His
words were literally meaningless. For if there was to be
no intervention to stop a genocide that was taking place,
then the phrase "Never again" meant nothing more than:
Never again would Germans kill Jews in Europe in the
1940s. Clinton might as well have said, "Never again the
potato famine," or "Never again the slaughter of the Albigensians." At the rate things were going, in the year 2050
could one expect that a future American President might
open a museum to ethnic cleansing?

During the 1992 election campaign, candidate Clinton had promised to use American power to bring this
Bosnian genocide to a halt (much later, a Clinton operative would exclaim to me in exasperation, "Why do people nowadays take campaign promises so seriously?"),

> The Europeans denied that any aggression had even taken place, and spoke instead of a civil war in Bosnia.

or, at least, give the Bosnian government the means to fight back. Two years later, Charles Redman, the US State Department official charged by President Clinton to come up with a peace plan for Bosnia, would justify American acceptance of the principle of partition by saying "we had to jump over the moral bridge" to obtain peace. At least the Americans remained committed rhetorically to the idea that the Bosnian government should be allowed to defend itself against Serb aggression, and, by late 1994, had decided they would no longer enforce the arms embargo. The Europeans denied that any aggression had even taken place, and spoke instead of a civil war in Bosnia. They steadfastly opposed lifting an arms embargo that the United Nations had passed more than a year earlier as part of a package of sanctions designed to penalize the Serbs for the war that they were waging against a secessionist Croatia. And they maintained this policy despite the fact that the war in Croatia had ended and it now served only to further the Serb cause in Bosnia. The Serbs and their Bosnian surrogates had more than enough arms. They had inherited the stores of the Yugoslav National Army. . . .

Leaving Bosnia to Fend for Itself

The real purpose of maintaining the embargo, of course, had long been to ensure that as few weapons as possible get through to the government side. Although the embargo had been passed by the United Nations Security Council on September 25, 1991, before Bosnia had declared its independence, the fact that only the Bosnian government was really affected troubled almost no one. To the British Foreign Secretary, Douglas Hurd, the military imbalance that the embargo perpetuated actually made it all the more important that the embargo remain in force. "We don't want to level the killing field," he said more than once. It seemed as if what Hurd was really afraid of was that if the Bosnian government forces were better armed they would give the Serbs a fight. Who knew what would happen then? Better, however unhappy such a choice might be, to wish for a Serb victory. At least the fighting would be over.

There were officials within the British government who were more than willing to concede as much. "We should never have accepted the dismemberment of Yugoslavia," wrote a Mr. R.D. Wilkinson of the Foreign Office Policy Planning Staff to the English conservative writer Nora Beloff, "without first having settled the problems of minorities and frontiers, and probably not before having put in hand a humane program of population exchange. The recognition of Bosnia, and indeed the incitement of them to proclaim their independence, was the ultimate act of thoughtlessness."

> All I could think of was the dead and how they need not have died.

In the American case, what seemed to be involved was an absolutely visceral reluctance to expend the political capital necessary to rescue Bosnia. "We can't let Bosnia endanger the best liberal hope for a generation," a former Colorado Senator and counselor to Clinton, Tim Wirth, was reported to have remarked. And disgruntled Clinton aides told the story that one critical moment when the administration was thinking of sending the Secretary of Defense to Sarajevo, Hillary Rodham Clinton argued passionately against the move on the grounds that this would take health care off the front page for the duration of his visit to Bosnia. Hearing these stories, all I could think of was the dead and how they need not have died. That simple thought still haunts me, whatever its effect might have been on the political fortunes of the best liberal hope for a generation.

The Serbs Held the Military Advantage

The effects of both Anglo-French hostility to Bosnia and American prevarication combined to ensure that throughout the two years of slaughter, it fell to the Bosnian government side to do the lion's share of the dying. Before the fighting began, the Serbs had almost all the guns (unlike Slovenia, Bosnia never established a territorial defense force and only created one after the shooting started), and after combat had begun in earnest, they were able to establish mainly untrammeled supply lines from Serbia proper, across Bosnia, and into Croatia. Ethnic cleansing was in part about making these routes secure from guerrilla attack. The Serbs also seized most of the high ground—the first axiom of military strategy. Whether we were contemplating the heights surrounding Sarajevo, or Mount Vlasic, in central Bosnia, with its commanding view of Muslim and Croat towns spread out below, those of us who spent the war mostly traveling with Bosnian government forces spent our time cowering under bombardment and with cricks in our necks from staring up at the gun positions on the other side. For all the publicity about bearded "Chetnik" irregulars, kitted out in Serbian white-eagle emblems, death's-head pins, and bandoliers of heavy machine-gun ammunition worn to make them look like the original Chetniks—the monarchist irregulars under the command of General Draja Mihailovic who had fought against Tito's partisans during the Second World War—most of the Serb fighters in Bosnia looked and acted like (and more often than not were) members of the regular JNA, the Yugoslav National Army. Before the Bosnian fighting had started, their commander, Ratko Mladic, had even commanded a corps during the Croatian war. It was only after the Serbs had conquered a third of Croatia that he had moved on to Pale, the Sarajevo suburb that served as the capital of the self-proclaimed Srpska Republika, the Serb Republic of Bosnia-Herzegovina. Mladic had acquired the rump of the JNA in Bosnia, its stores and cantonments as well as most of its regular officers and men, and it showed. "The Serbs are real soldiers," a Canadian officer serving with UN forces in Sarajevo told me in the early winter of 1993. "Whatever you think of what they've done, to me they're a known quantity."

That their main accomplishment was, in fact, murder, albeit murder with carefully thought-out political and military goals—ethnic cleansing was not just a war crime, it was a tactic for holding captured territory without having to worry about a restive subject population—seemed, to the mounting frustration of the journalists covering the fighting and the UN's role in relieving its effects but not interceding in it, to matter not at all. To the average officer in UNPROFOR—the acronym, much derided on the Bosnian side, where the word "self" was added before "protection," stood for United Nations Protection Force—the atmosphere in the officers' mess in Pale was not, making a few allowances for war conditions and Balkan peculiarities, all that different from that of the mess halls in which he was accustomed to taking his meals or relaxing. In contrast, Bosnian government officers tended to be civilians learning on the job how to be soldiers. They slouched in their chairs, walked with decidedly non-military gaits, and gave the impression of being utterly innocent of the various rituals and conventions that lie at the heart of the military vocation in almost every country. Many if not most of them had been civilians, the rest junior officers. Certainly, it was rare to meet a senior officer serving with Bosnia government forces who, before the war, had held a commission above the rank of major in the JNA.

Bosnians Could Not Believe What Was Happening

What the Bosnians did have was their illusions, particularly their belief that what had been happening to them

A woman in a danger-ous suburb of Sarajevo walks defiantly by an armed soldier during the siege of 1993. Yugoslavs had a hard time believing that such a prosperous European country could fall into war so quickly. **(Tom Stoddart/Getty Images.)**

since the killing had started was somehow a kind of ghastly category mistake. It was as if, in a kind of mir-ror image of [UN secretary-general Boutros] Boutros-Ghali's dismissive sketch of their predicament, Bosnians imagined that the fact that they were Europeans would protect them from the horrors of war. Europe, for them, was a continent in which the cosmopolitan values they stood for had become the norm. In Sarajevo, in par-ticular, up to almost the very moment the fighting broke out, the expectation had been that life in the future there would not be very different from life in other genteel, provincial European cities—Trieste, say, or Graz. Even when they realized they were cruelly mistaken about what the future held in store for them, few managed to entirely jettison these expectations. Wars were not supposed to take place in the hardwood forests of Europe in the 1990s, between people for whom the ownership of seaside cottages, second cars, and university educations had become commonplace. Wars occurred in the poor world. In a rich country such as the former Yugoslavia, its sanguinary history notwithstanding, a well-appointed, civilized peace was supposed to reign.

When war had come, the urban middle class of Bosnia, particularly in the cities of Sarajevo, Mostar, Tuzla, and Banja Luka, painfully came to realize that although they had listened to the speeches of Serb nationalists like Slobodan Milosevic, the President of Serbia, and Radovan Karadzic, the leader of the Bosnian Serbs, in truth they had heard nothing. Comparisons between Milosevic and Hitler are foolish and unworthy—the knee-jerk impulse of an age mired in rhetorical excess which has to insist that anything good is the greatest and anything bad the worst—but this Sarajevan inability to hear *is* reminiscent of the reaction of Karl Kraus, that paradigmatic Central European cosmopolitan of the interwar period, who wrote, "When I think of Hitler, nothing comes to mind." Even today so many cosmopolitan Sarajevans cannot quite take in what happened to them. It is this cognitive dissonance, this misunderstanding of their own historical situation, that has differentiated the Bosnian reaction to the war that engulfed them from that of Afghans or Angolans. In Bosnia, the universal pain that all wars engender has carried with it that tinge of surprise of those who believed that their material lives would always be happy. So much for the

> Wars were not supposed to take place . . . between people for whom the ownership of seaside cottages, second cars, and university education had become commonplace.

notion that the end of history, which was never anything more than the end of communism, would be followed by a dull and pacifying age of consumerism.

Experiencing the Unthinkable

I think now that I believed it too, imagining that for white Europeans at least, the sanguinary epochs had ended definitively. I knew that, historically, Europe had not been an especially benign place and that in certain periods—like the first fifty years of the twentieth century, to name the one I should have been paying attention to— it had been a particularly *savage* place. But if I knew this, I did not believe it viscerally, whatever pieties I had been capable of uttering about Hiroshima and Auschwitz, the ruin of Africa and the Gulag archipelago. Those events might as well have taken place in another geological era. The crisis looming in Europe, I had thought before I started going to Bosnia, would revolve around the generalized global servant crisis that the rich world seemed to be going through.

In ever larger numbers, people from the poor, non-European world were successfully migrating to the countries of the European Union and North America, to do the jobs that the native-born were no longer willing to take on. It was the presence of these immigrants, and the challenges—cultural, racial, and linguistic—that they posed, which seemed to me the great, intractable dilemma that the future held in store for the rich world. That such a transformation was bound to create a crisis was self-evident. Europe had no tradition of immigration; unlike the United States, which was undergoing its own immigration-driven transformation, there was no powerful cognitive context for what was going on. But a crisis did not mean a war, although, in my bleaker moments, I found it easy to imagine a future Europe in which repression and radical de-democratization had become the norm. *That* Europe would be made up of citizens and immigrants. In other words, as a society it would be closer to slaveholding Athens than to the Social Democratic world of the post-1945, pre-1989 Western European consensus. But what I could not imagine was the sound of tank fire, and the ping of sniper's bullets resounding through the windows of high rises, across the neat parks, the supermarkets, and the gleaming cafes, the art galleries, auto-body repair shops, and historic centers, of a city like Sarajevo. I could not imagine these things any more than the Bosnians themselves could imagine them, before the unthinkable engulfed them.

A War Reporter Struggles to Remember and to Forget the Siege of Sarajevo

Janine di Giovanni

In the following selection, a war reporter recalls the horrors and deprivations of life during wartime in Sarajevo. She describes her return fifteen years after the conflict, when she reconnected with her Serb protector, a man who sided with Bosnian forces. She notes the devastating impact the war has had on him. They revisit where she, under fire, reported on the conflict, and where his side fought in the streets with Serb gunmen. In a city that changed so much in the years after the war, they struggle to remember—while also wishing to forget—the details. Janine di Giovanni, who has covered conflict in various parts of the globe since the 1980s, has written six books and numerous articles.

SOURCE. Janine di Giovanni, "The Book of the Dead," *Granta*, v. 111, Summer 2010, pp. 37–53. Used by permission of the author, on behalf of Inkwell Management.

My home on the fourth floor of the Holiday Inn on Sniper's Alley [in Sarajevo] had plastic windows that came from UNHCR [UN High Commissioner for Refugees] aid packets. On one side of the ugly, Communist-era room was my flak jacket and my helmet with my blood group taped to it. On my shrapnel-chipped desk was a battery-operated Tandy, a high-street precursor to a laptop, a flashlight, a box of candles, four lighters, a box of chocolates and three bottles of water.

Life in Sarajevo During the War

Physically, I was deteriorating. I had grown accustomed to not washing and I wore the same clothes several days in a row. Oddly enough, even though no one washed in those days, no one seemed to smell. Once a week, I bribed the men who guarded the hotel kitchen with a few packs of Marlboro Lights for a pot of hot water, and with that, I would set aside an hour to wash my hair. One night, in a fit of despair, I had chopped off my long thick hair with a pair of borrowed manicure scissors and although I looked odd, it made my life easier.

My view out of the plastic window was of a wasted, gutted city of burnt-out buildings and metal canisters that were used to deter the snipers. It was so cold that my skin peeled off when I took off my layers of clothes. I was living on a diet of chocolate bars I had brought in from Kiseljak—the Las Vegas frontier town that was the last stop before besieged Sarajevo—whisky, vitamins and cigarettes.

To this day, I cannot forget that cold. My internal barometer changed forever. The large, cavernous, Soviet-style unheated rooms where we would interview doctors or politicians; the freezing cold houses where people sat huddled and frightened around an oil stove; the ugly interior of the lobby of the Holiday Inn, where one afternoon I came back to see journalists abseiling down from the roof with ropes. Ice-crusted, breathing out slow breaths of frozen air.

I shivered when I woke in my sleeping bag, I shivered when I climbed out and slipped into the same clothes on the floor, and I shivered climbing back into the bag at night, to read by candlelight. Bizarrely, uniformed maids came every day to make up the beds—that is, to pat down the sleeping bags and to move around the dust. There was not much they could do without water. The toilets did not flush and nothing came out of the taps.

> The worst was the knowledge that I could leave whenever I wanted to, and they could not.

I was mentally fried. Every day people came to me with some kind of request: get me out of here, take a package to my sister, take my child to Germany, give me some money for firewood. There was only so much I could physically do in one day, and when I did not, Catholic guilt preyed on me ferociously.

The worst was the knowledge that I could leave whenever I wanted to, and they could not. My friend Corinne kept reminding me I was not a social worker but a journalist. But for all of us living in that place, that time, it was impossible not to blur the lines. . . .

Back in Sarajevo, 2010

Louie was a soldier, and my friend. A tall, thin Serb from Sarajevo who fought on the Bosnian side. He was my unofficial bodyguard, a big brother, a protector. He was never a comforter—too gruff for that—but he was someone I knew I could trust with my life. He says, "No one ever touched you during the war because of me."

In those days, when I would fall into deep despair, out of fear or loneliness or isolation or sorrow, he would take me to strange places with strange people—gangsters, probably—where they had a bottle of whisky. Then we would smoke and drink, and he would say, "Feel better? Now go home." He would drive me home and walk me to my door. He never touched me, although he loved women.

When I see him now, he is so much, much older. He shakes. He drinks a lot. He carries a sadness that I know you cannot wash away, or scour clean, the way the nuns in the orphanage did.

What is it you saw? What did you taste, what did you smell? Those first days of war when you and your friends tried to hold off the tanks with Kalashnikovs, when you gathered at a factory out near the airport, a small virtually helpless band of boy Davids trying to fight off Goliath—what did you think?

Louie and I return on my last day in the new Sarajevo to all the places of the dead. To the front lines where he fought, eighteen years ago. He has never been back, and at some moments while we stare silently at the buildings where he crouched with a gun, at the factory where the battle raged for more than twenty-four hours, I am thinking perhaps it was not a good idea to bring him back.

"My nerves," he says to me. "Now you wonder why I shake so much?"

We stand on a railway bridge in Otes, a suburb of Sarajevo, and he looks like he will cry: we had no guns, he says quietly, we had only rifles that cost a hundred Deutschmarks and we tried to take the guns from the dead soldiers . . . We look down at a muddy, polluted creek, and I can still see the dead bodies, floating, bloated.

At the Jewish cemetery, the scene of some of the heaviest fighting, where the men fought from headstone to headstone, someone has built a new house. A sparkling *Architectural Digest* house that leans out over the city heights, with a view of Sarajevo below. It's someone who was not here during the war of course—if he was, he would not live here, among so many dead, so many lingering dead.

Then we go to Dobrinja. It was a wild place, a suburb cut off from the rest of the city for most of the war, where the fighting was always intense. I remember days of shelling, of sitting with people screaming from fear and pain, of running across fields of snow with soldiers urging me to run faster, run faster, reporter run faster . . .

> "When we go back . . . neither of us can [recognize] anything."

In Dobrinja—where transporters opened up on the civilians on 4 May 1992 and a loudspeaker urged the people to take hand luggage and leave (not many of the population of 45,000 did), Louie fought hand to hand. He was what they called a defender of the city.

But when we go back, there is a terrible moment when neither of us can remember anything. We go back to the main street—now called Branilaca Dobrinje—Defenders of Dobrinja—but we can't recognize our old landmarks. We grope like the blind, trying to feel, trying to recall, trying to pull out of our memories what happened.

Instead of a wasted, grey outlay of Communist-style buildings eaten away by tank shells and dead faces, and people running from snipers, there are pizza parlours, a playground, gold shops, gangs of beautiful teenagers smoking cigarettes, a sports hall and dogs rolling in the early-spring sun.

"My God," Louie says. His eyes tear up. "I can't remember anything. I can't see where we were . . ." He climbs out of his car and lights a cigarette. He is growing agitated. He is shaking again. He stares and stares at the buildings, looking a little desperate. And I remember what I once asked my husband, who also survived many wars:

"Did this stuff, this war stuff, f--- us up?"

"How could it not?" he answered.

I can't remember anything in Dobrinja either. I can't recognize where we once stood together, in the cold, in

the winter, in the summer. I can't remember the tanks. But wait—isn't that the building I sprinted from with a soldier who was taking me to the front line, holding my hand as we ran? No, it can't be. And isn't that basement the old Bosnian Army headquarters? The room where I saw that ancient woman who was dying of the cold? The place where the children were killed . . . the snow banks, the trenches, the sandbags used as defences, the metal canisters . . .

Workers rebuild and repair damaged houses in Sarajevo after the siege. **(Tom Stoddart Archive/Getty Images.)**

Everything has changed. Everything and nothing.

"Let's go," Louie says quietly. "I don't want to remember, anyway."

CHRONOLOGY

1100s	The kingdom of Bosnia takes shape.
1463	Ottoman Turks conquer the region.
1878	Austria-Hungary begins administering Bosnia and annexes it in 1908.
1914	On June 28, a young Bosnian Serb, Gavrilo Princip, assassinates Austrian archduke Franz Ferdinand in Sarajevo, Bosnia—an event that helps set off World War I.
1918	After WWI, a new Kingdom of Serbs, Croats, and Slovenes is created that includes Bosnia.
1929	The kingdom is renamed Yugoslavia.
1941–43	During World War II, the conquering Nazis establish a puppet Independent State of Croatia and make Bosnia part of it.
1943–45	After defeating the Nazis, a Communist leader, Josip Broz (known as Tito), establishes a socialist Yugoslavia made up of six centrally controlled republics: Bosnia, Serbia, Croatia, Slovenia, Macedonia, and Montenegro.
1980	Tito dies on May 4 and central control of Yugoslavia begins to unravel.
1983	Authorities imprison Bosnia Muslim activist Alija Izetbegovic, who sought multiparty democracy. He

serves five years. Two years after his release, he becomes
president of Bosnia, in office for most of the next
decade.

1984   The Winter Olympic Games are held in Sarajevo,
Bosnia's central city.

1987   Slobodan Milosevic assumes control of Serbia, empha-
sizing Serb rights. Over the next few years he gains
influence in other regions of Yugoslavia as well.

1990   In Bosnia's first open elections, the Izetbegovic's Muslim
party wins 26.6 percent of the vote, the new Serbian
party led by Radovan Karadzic wins 23.5 percent, and
a mainly Croatian party wins 14.4 percent. The three
form a coalition government.

1991   Milosevic and the new leader of Croatia, Franjo
Tudjman, reportedly agree to divide Bosnia between
them.

1991   Croatia and Slovenia declare themselves independent
countries in June. Over several months, Croatian forces
fight elements of the Yugoslav army and Serbs declaring
autonomy.

1992   February: Bosnians vote for independence from
Yugoslavia, though many Bosnian Serbs boycott the
election.

March: As independence is being declared in Bosnia,
Bosnian Serb armed groups begin attacking non-Serbs
and government installations. This is the beginning of
armed conflict that will go on for about three and a half
years.

April 5: Serb forces begin a siege of Sarajevo, Bosnia's

mountain-ringed capital, that lasts until the end of February 1996.

April–May: The United Nations, the United States, and the European Community recognize Bosnia, Croatia, and Slovenia as independent nations.

May: In Bosnia, after taking over several towns, Serb forces begin a four-year siege of the city of Gorazde. The Bosnian Serb Army, known as VRS, is formed, led by Ratko Mladic.

May 27: The VRS shells civilians in a Sarajevo marketplace, killing twenty and wounding one hundred people.

May 30: The UN Security Council imposes economic sanctions on what remains of Yugoslavia, which is run by Milosevic.

July–August: Western journalists report that non-Serb Bosnians have been victims of large-scale atrocities.

December: The US Secretary of State calls for the prosecution of Serbs, including Milosevic and Karadzic, for war crimes.

1993   March: The United States begins airlifting supplies to besieged Bosnians.

April: In addition to struggles with Serbian forces, Bosnian government fighters begin battling armed Bosnian Croats.

May–August: The Serb VRS makes military gains in Bosnian territory.

May 25: The United Nations creates an international tribunal for war crimes in the former Yugoslavia. The tribunal is based in The Hague, The Netherlands. It is apparent that all sides in the conflict are committing atrocities, and the fighting grows in complexity.

November 8: The high-arch stone bridge in the Bosnian city of Mostar, built in 1566 as a symbol of cultural diversity, is destroyed.

1994 February 5: An artillery shell from a Serb position kills sixty-eight people and wounds hundreds in a Sarajevo outdoor market.

March: With US mediation, Croats and Muslims in Bosnia reach a cease-fire agreement. Serb-Muslim warfare continues.

April: NATO bombs Serb positions around Gorazde.

1995 July: About eight thousand Muslim men and boys are massacred in the Bosnian city of Srebrenica, which had been declared a civilian haven by the United Nations.

August: NATO air strikes hit Serb positions.

October: A cease-fire begins in Bosnia, supervised by NATO troops.

November: Talks begin in Dayton, Ohio, to settle the conflict. US assistant secretary of state Richard Holbrooke mediates among the presidents of Bosnia, Serbia, and Croatia.

December: The Dayton agreement is formally signed in Paris. It divides Bosnia into Serbian and non-Serb sectors under a central government. A largely American force of sixty thousand NATO peacekeepers deploys in Bosnia to enforce the agreement.

1998   UN war crimes tribunal convictions include Bosnian Muslims and Croats.

1999   In March, NATO bombs targets in Serbia, including the capital, Belgrade, and in the disputed territory of Kosovo, as conflicts persist in the regions bordering Bosnia to the south and east.

2000   After Milosevic is voted out as president of Yugoslavia (Serbia) in December, he is arrested on corruption charges and turned over to the UN war crimes tribunal.

2001   The UN war crimes tribunal convicts a Bosnian Serb general, Radislav Krstic, of aiding and abetting genocide in the Srebrenica deaths in July 1995. His forty-six-year sentence is later reduced on appeal to thirty-five years.

2004   The Mostar bridge, rebuilt with the help of funds from UNESCO, reopens July 24.

2006   Milosevic, on trial at the war crimes tribunal, dies of heart failure March 11.

2008   Karadzic is detained and turned over to the tribunal in July. His trial begins more than a year later, then is delayed six months while Karadzic refuses to attend. The trial resumes March 1, 2010, without any sign of when it will end.

FOR FURTHER READING

Books

Sidney Blumenthal, *The Clinton Wars*. New York: Farrar, Straus and Giroux, 2003.

Steven L. Burg and Paul S. Shoup, *The War in Bosnia-Herzegovina: Ethnic Conflict and International Intervention*. Armonk, NY: M.E. Sharpe, 2000.

Central Intelligence Agency, *Balkan Battlegrounds: A Military History of the Yugoslav Conflict, 1990–1995*. Washington, DC: Central Intelligence Agency, Office of Public Affairs, 2002.

Derek Chollet, *The Road to the Dayton Accords: A Study of American Statecraft*. London: Palgrave Macmillan, 2005.

Roger Cohen, *Hearts Grown Brutal: Sagas of Sarajevo*. New York: Random House, 1998.

Elizabeth M. Cousens and Charles K. Cater, *Toward Peace in Bosnia: Implementing the Dayton Accords*. Boulder: Lynne Rienner, 2001.

Bogdan Denitch, *Ethnic Nationalism: The Tragic Death of Yugoslavia*. Minneapolis: University of Minnesota Press, 1994.

Andre Gerolymatos, *The Balkan Wars: Conquest, Revolution, and Retribution from the Ottoman Era to the Twentieth Century and Beyond*. New York: Basic Books, 2003.

Pierce Hazan, *Justice in a Time of War: The True Story Behind the International Criminal Tribunal for the Former Yugoslavia*. College Station: Texas A&M University Press, 2004.

Mira Markovic, *Night and Day: A Diary*. Kingston, ON: Quarry Press, 1996.

Nader Mousavizadeh, ed., *The Black Book of Bosnia: The Consequences of Appeasement*. New York: Basic Books, 1996.

David Owen, *Balkan Odyssey*. New York: Harcourt Brace, 1995.

Mirko Pejanovic, *Through Bosnian Eyes: The Political Memoirs of a Bosnian Serb*. Sarajevo: Sahinpasic, 2002.

Richard J. Samuels, ed., "Bosnia Intervention," *Encyclopedia of US National Security*, vol. 1, pp. 87–89. Thousand Oaks, CA: Sage Reference, 2006.

Laura Silber and Allan Little, *Yugoslavia: The Death of a Nation*. London: Penguin Books/BBC Books, 1996.

John S. Sray, *US Policy and the Bosnian Civil War: A Time for Reevaluation*. Washington, DC: Foreign Military Studies Office, 1995.

Mark Thompson, *A Paper House: The Ending of Yugoslavia*. New York: Pantheon Books, 1992.

Warren Zimmermann, *Origins of a Catastrophe: Yugoslavia and Its Destroyers*. New York: Times Books, 1996.

Periodicals

Syed Abid Ali, "The Intractable Bosnian Conflict: An Appraisal," *Economic Review*, vol. 25, no. 1, January 1994, pp. 7–8.

American Spectator, "At Dawn to Cast His Flies," October 1993, p. 14.

Christopher Bennett, "No Flying Colors for Dayton—Yet," *Transitions*, December 1997, p. 37.

Anthony Borden, Slavenka Drakulic, and George Kenny, "Bosnia's Democratic Charade," *Nation*, vol. 263, no. 8, September 23, 1996, pp. 14–18.

Ted Galen Carpenter and Amos Perlmutter, "Strategy Creep in the Balkans: Up to Our Knees and Advancing," *National Interest*, no. 44, Summer 1996, pp. 53–59.

Jonathan G. Clarke, "America Should Stay Out of Future Bosnias," *USA Today Magazine*, vol. 124, no. 2612, May 1996, pp. 22–24.

Bill Clinton, "The Risk of 'Americanizing' the War," *Newsweek*, vol. 126, no. 6, August 7, 1995, p. 40.

Alexander Cockburn, "Beat the Devil," *Nation*, vol. 258, no. 20, May 23, 1994, pp. 692–693.

Robert M. Hayden, "Bosnia: The Contradictions of 'Democracy' Without Consent," *East European Constitutional Review*, vol. 7, Spring 1998, pp. 37–51.

Christopher Hitchens, "Letter from America," *New Statesman & Society*, vol. 6, no. 279, November 19, 1993, p. 11.

Samuel P. Huntington, "The Clash of Civilizations," *Foreign Affairs*, vol. 72, Summer 1993, pp. 22–49.

Andrew Kohut and Robert C. Toth, "Arms and the People," *Foreign Affairs*, vol. 73, no. 6, November–December 1994, pp. 47–61.

John J. Mearsheimer and Robert A. Pape, "The Answer," *New Republic*, June 14, 1993, pp. 22–29.

National Review, "Bosnian Bog," vol. 46, no. 22, November 21, 1994, pp. 22–23.

Progressive, "The Menace of War," vol. 59, no. 9, September 1995, p. 8.

Yahya M. Sadowski, "Bosnia's Muslims: A Fundamentalist Threat?" *Brookings Review*, vol. 13, no. 1, Winter 1995, pp. 10–15.

Wall Street Journal, "The West May Have Its Man in Bosnia," June 28, 2000, p. A16.

INDEX

A

Abortions, 108, 111
Albanians, 33, 82–83
Albright, Madeleine, 149
Armenians, 187
Arms embargo, 96–97, 99, 101, 186

B

Babic, Milan, 51
Baker, James, *82*, 87–88
Balkans. *See* Yugoslavia; specific countries
Bassiouni, M. Cherif, 103–114
Bert, Wayne, 93–102
Bildt, Carl, 155
Black market activities, 68
Bosnia-Herzegovina
European Union (EU) recognition, 16,
91, 92
independence, 68, 91
joint presidency, 19–20
map, *16*
Yugoslavia's breakup, 26
Bosnian conflict
casualties, 39, 43, 48, 49, 68, 134
economic causes, 60–70
historically, 21–26
humanitarian aid, 27–33, 43
imperialism and, 136–140
religious causes, 71–79
United States and, 63, 79–92, 88, 151–
159
See also Sarajevo

Boutros-Ghali, Boutros, 90, 190
Brune, Lester H., 79–92
Bush, George H.W., 80, 84, 86, 88, 92, 96,
100, 156
Byzantine Empire, 21–22

C

Camps
concentration camps, 38, 77, 85
detention camps, 38, 77, 85, 105, 106
rape camps, 107–110
refugee camps, *130*
Canada, 129
Carrington, Lord, 90–91
Cemeteries, 172–174, 197–198, *See also*
mass graves
Chetniks, 188
Chirac, Jacques, 131
CIA (Central Intelligence Agency), 86, 129
Claes, Willy, 129, 132–133
Clinton, Bill
Dayton Accords and, 34, 80, 159
imperialism and, 138–140
photograph, *35*
Srebrenica massacre and, 130
Thatcher's letter and, 27, 28
US Holocaust Museum and, 184, 185
US intervention in Bosnia and, 187
US nonintervention and, 80, 95,
99–100, 187
US peacemaking efforts, 34–45
Clinton, Hillary Rodham, 187

Cold War, 26, 37, 40, 65–66, 80, 101–102, 152–153

Communism
  in the Balkans, 26, 32, 37, 66, 156
  end of, 80, 152, 192
  See also Cold War, Tito, Soviet Union

Concentration camps, 38, 77, 85

Croatia
  casualties, 48, 49
  ethnic cleansing, 32
  European Union (EU) recognition, 91, 92
  Germany and, 138
  independence and, 68, 86
  Nazis and, 14, 24
  religion, 22
  Yugoslavia's breakup, 4, 26
  See also Tudjman; Yugoslavia

Cusack, Michael, 21–26

Cutileiro, Jose, 91

D

D'Amato, Alfonse, 86

Dayton Accords
  Clinton and, 34, 80, 161
  human rights and, 19, 39
  implementation, 158–159
  NATO peacekeepers and, 134–135
  Operation Deliberate Force and, 134
  peace negotiations, 17, 39
  photograph, *154*

Delors, Jacques, 87

DeMichelis, Gianni, 88

Detention camps, 38, 77, 85, 105, 106

Di Giovanni, Janine, 194–200

Dizdarevic, Zlatko, 169–181

Dodok, Milorad, 56

Dole, Robert, 86

Dutch UN troops, 119–120

Dubrovnik, Croatia, 48, 90

E

Eagleburger, Lawrence, 81, 84, 87, 97, 157

Eastern Orthodox Church, 21–22, 24, 49, 74

Electricity outages, 117, 164, 165, 174, 176

Embargoes
  arms embargo, 96–97, 99, 101, 128, 186
  Serbian embargo of Slovenian trade, 84

Ethnic cleansing
  cultural cleansing, 72–73
  development of term, 18, 49
  military goals, 189
  perpetrators, 16, 157
  rape and, 113
  religion and, 75–78
  United Nations and, 28–29
  world response, 32
  See also Muslims; Religion

European Union (EU)
  Bosnia-Herzegovina recognition, 16, 91, 92
  Bosnian conflict and, 63
  Bush and, 80
  Croatia recognition, 91, 92
  humanitarian aid and, 29
  Serbia and, 16, 53
  Slovenia recognition, 92
  Yugoslavia break-up and, 87

F

Filipović, Zlata, 161–169

Food shortages, 117, 164, *175*, 177–178, 181

France
  European Council and, 85

imperialism, 137
NATO bombing flights, 132t
UN peacekeepers, 89, 90, 118t, 129
World War II Allies, 23, 24
Franz Ferdinand, Crown Prince of Austria, 14, 23, *25*
Fuel, 177–178, 180

G

Geneva Conventions, 185
Genocide, 18, 24, 51, 53, 55, 148, 184–185
Germany, 24, 85, 137, 138, 157, 184, 196
Goldstone, Richard J., 50–51, 141–150
Gorbachev, Mikhail, 83
Great Britain, *See* United Kingdom
Greece, 23, 82

H

The Hague, 51, 57, 90, 148, 149
Havel, Vaclav, 158
Hendrickson, Ryan C., 126–135
Hitler, Adolph, 49, 142, 153, 156
Holbrooke, Richard, 132, 151–159
Holocaust, 184, 185
Hospitals, 163, 170–172, 178
Human rights
    Albanians and, 82–83
    Dayton Accords and, 19, 39
    European Union (EU) recognition and, 90
    international intervention, 61
    Reagan and, 81
    South Africa and, 145
    strategic interests and, 155–158
Humanitarian aid, 27–33, 43, 70, 127, 177–178
Humiliation, 96, 102, 107, 110–111, 113

Hungary, 23, 33, 82
Hurd, Douglas, 87, 186–187

I

Imperialism, 136–140
International Monetary Fund (IMF), 81, 83
International War Crimes Tribunal, 19, 47, 53, 56, 141–150, *143*
Iraq, 30, 127, 137
Islam, *See* Muslims
Italy, 137, 184
Izetbegovic, Alija, 14, 87, 91, 140, *154*

J

Jansa, Janez, 88–89
Janvier, Bernard, 119, 131–132
Jews, 24, 73, 184
JNA (Yugoslav National Army), 186, 188–189
John Paul II, Pope, 45

K

Karadzic, Radovan
    middle-class response, 191
    Republika Srpska leadership and, 91
    war crimes, 19, 146, 148
Kidnapping, 50, 106, 111
Kosovo
    arms embargo and, 96
    ethnic cleansing and, 33
    history, 49
    human rights and, 82
    Kosovo conflict, 98, 134, 135
    photograph, *139*
Kuchan, Milan, 83, 84, 87
Kuwait, 30, 32, 127

L

Lion's Graveyard, 172–174

Looting, 105

M

Macedonia, 33, 96, 134–135

Malaysia, 118t

Markovic, Ante, 83–90

Mass graves, 38, 105

McCormick, Marcia, 103–114

Militant (newspaper), 136–140

Milosevic, Slobodan
  Baker and, 87
  blame for Bosnian conflict, 63, 139
  cease-fire violation, 89
  Dayton Accords and, 17, 125
  death, 46–51
  deception, 32
  EU recognition of Bosnia and, 91
  family, 50, 51
  human rights and, 83
  Kosovo and, 135
  nationlism and, 81
  personality, 50
  photographs, *47, 154*
  rise to power, 144, 193
  Slovenian embargo and, 84
  Vance's cease-fire proposal and, 90–91
  war crimes and, 19, 146, 148

Mladic, Ratko, 19, 51, 53, 56–58, 124, 146, 188–189

Monnet, Jean, 153

Montenegro, 26, 128

Muslim-Croat federation, 16, 18–20

Muslims
  bombing of cultural archives and, 74
  casualties, 49, 68
  cultural cleansing and, 72–73
  ethnic cleansing and, 75–78
  ghettos, 29–30
  massacres, 120–122, 124, 130, 146–147
  mosque destruction, *77*
  Ottoman Empire invasion of Bosnia, 22
  See also Ethnic cleansing; Religion

N

Nationalism, 63, 81, 157

NATO (North Atlantic Treaty Organization)
  bombing campaign, 16–17, 126–135, 132t, 179
  creation, 40
  Dayton Accords and, 19
  I-FOR (international force) for peace, 41–45
  imperialism and, 136–140
  Kosovo and, 98, 135
  Kuwait and, 30
  peacekeeping force, *12,* 13, 134–135
  Russia and, 153
  United States and, 39, 41

Nazis, 14, 24, 80, 184

Netherlands, 88, 118t

Nickles Amendment, 86, 87

O

Operation Deliberate Force, 127, 131–135

Organization for Security and Cooperation in Europe (OSCE), 153

Ottoman Empire, 22–23

Owen, David (Lord), 96

Owen, Robert C., 133

P

Pakistan, 118t

Personal stories
    girl in Sarajevo, 161–168
    Sarajevo newspaper editor, 172–181
    U.S. journalist, 182–193
    war reporter, 194–200
Poos, Jacques, 88, 89
Powell, Colin, 88
Public transportation, 174–175

R

Radio Belgrade, 49
Radio France Internationale (FRI), 167
Radio Free Europe/Radio Liberty, 55
Rape
    forced impregnation, 108–109, 111–112
    gang rape, 106, 107, 111
    military leadership and, 112–113
    public rape, 106, 111
    rape camps, 107–110
    war tactics and, 103–114
Raznatovic, Zeljko (Arkan), 125
Reagan, Ronald, 81, 156
Realpolitik, 32, 155
Refugee camps, *130*
Religion
    cause for Bosnian conflict, 71–79
    Eastern Orthodox Church, 21–22, 24,
      49, 74
    ethnic cleansing and, 75–78
    Kosovo as religious site, 98
    Roman Catholicism, 22, 73, 77, 105,
      109, 111
    See also Ethnic cleansing; Muslims
Republika Srpska
    capital, 190
    creation, 91
    Dayton Accords and, 19
    elections, 20

genocide and, 56
Rieff, David, 184–195
Russia, 21–23, 80, 101, 134, 153

S

Sarajevo, Bosnia-Herzgovina
    Franz Ferdinand assassination and, 14
    Lion's Graveyard, 172–174
    Olympics, 44
    personal stories, 161–181
    photographs, *12, 64, 167, 190*
    rebuilding, 198, *199*
    siege of Sarajevo, 29–31, 68, 91, 146
    U.S. soldiers and, *97*
    war crimes and, 185–186
Sarajevo Haggadah, 73
Sarajevo National Library, *59*, 60, 72
Schools, 170
Sells, Michael A., 71–79
Serbia
    economic sanctions, 38, 128
    ethnic cleansing, 32
    European Union (EU) membership, 53
    genocide of Serbs during WWII, 24
    history, 24, 49
    US air power and, 30–31
    Yugoslavia's breakup, 26
Slovenia
    European Union (EU) recognition, 92
    religion and, 22
    Yugoslavia break-up and, 26, 84, 86,
      88–89, 188
Somalia, 129, 137
Soviet Union, 23, 33, 63, 152, 154, *See also*
  Cold War, Communism, Russia
Spain, 73, 118t
Srebrenica massacre, 52–58, *54*, 115–125,
  130, 147–148, *160*

Synovitz, Ron, 52–58

T

Tadic, Boris, 56
Tanner, Marcus, 46–51
Telephone system, 176–177
Thatcher, Margaret, 27–33, *28*
Tito, Josip Broz, 14, *17*, 24, 81, 188
Truman, Harry S., 154
Tudjman, Franjo

Baker and, 87
Croatian leaders, 81, 83
Eagleburger and, 84
ethnic cleansing and, 139
Holocaust and, 184
photograph, *154*
Serb-Croat conflict and, 89, 95
Yugoslavian unity and, 84, 87
Turkey, 82, 118t

U

UN High Commissioner for Refugees (UNHCR), 119, 125
UN Protection Force (UNPROFOR)
cease-fire agreements and, 32, 90, 91
endangerment, 31, 95
humanitarian aid and, 127
passive role, 101–102
Srebrenica and, 117–120
withdrawal from Bosnia, 99
United Kingdom
Bosnian children evacuations, 179
European Council and, 85
UN peacekeepers, 90, 118t
imperialism, 137
NATO bombing flights 132t
World War II Allies, 23, 24

United Nations (UN)
casualties, 128
embargoes and, 186–187
evacuation of troops from Bosnia, 131
humanitarian aid, 28–29, 70, 127
peacekeeping efforts, 16, 24–26, 89, 116, 131–132
war crimes tribunal, 19, 47, 53, 56
United States
air power, 30–31, 38
Bosnia-Herzegovina recognition, 91
casualties, 129
ethnic conflicts, 69–70
humanitarian aid, 29
imperialism and, 136–140
mishandling of Bosnian conflict, 63, 79–92
NATO and, 39, 41, 130
NATO bombing flights, 132t
nonintervention policy for Bosnia, 88, 93–102
peace facilitation, 34–45
World War II and, 36
Ustache, 24–25

V

Van den Broek, Hans, 88
Vance, Cyrus, 90–91, 97

Vance-Owen peace plan, 95
Vietnam Syndrome, 88, 102

W

War crimes, *See* International War Crimes Tribunal, Koradzic
Water shortages, 176, 178, 181, 196
Wiesel, Elie, 184, 185
Wilson, Woodrow, 152, 155, 156

Woodward, Susan L., 60–70

World Bank, 81, 83

World War I, 14, 23, 36–37, 152

World War II
    concentration camps, 38
    Croatia and, 14, 24
    ethnic hatred and, 156
    Jews and, 73
    refugees and, 16
    United States and, 36, 156

Worldmark Encyclopedia of the Nations, 13–20

Y

YNA/YPA (Yugoslav National Army/People's Army), 89–91, 116

Yugoslavia
    breakup, 26, 84, 86–89, 188
    Cold War and, 65–66
    communism and, 158
    countries making up Yugoslavia, 14
    ethnic populations, 23t
    formation, 25
    history, 22
    inflation rates 1979–1991, 67t
    map, 15
    overview of conflict, 13–20
    Russian influence, 22–23
    See also specific countries

Z

Zimmermann, Warren, 81–84, 86–87, 91